A Reluctant Pioneer

JoEllen Collins

STRATTON
—PRESS—
Publishing Life

A RELUCTANT PIONEER
Copyright © 2021 **JoEllen Collins**

Stratton Press Publishing
831 N Tatnall Street Suite M #188,
Wilmington, DE 19801
www.stratton-press.com
1-888-323-7009

ISBN (Paperback): 978-1-64895-328-6
ISBN (Ebook): 978-1-64895-329-3

Printed in the United States of America

When You Are Old

William Butler Yeats

When you are old and gray and full of sleep,
And nodding by the fire, take down this book,
And slowly read, and dream of the soft look
Your eyes had once, and of their shadows deep.

How many loved your moments of glad grace,
And loved your beauty with love false or true;
But one man loved the pilgrim soul in you,
And loved the sorrows of your changing face.

And bending down beside the glowing bars,
Murmur, a little sadly, how love fled
And paced upon the mountains overhead
And hid his face amid a crowd of stars.

To all my women friends

Chapter One

H idden behind bushes of blackberries, the small plot of graves seemed only a brief hyphen in the vastness of the landscape around it. A large deodar tree shadowed the clearing. If Leah hadn't known of its existence, she would probably have walked by it, but now she knelt down to wipe off the dirt from the two small granite stones.

One read:

Helen Ingrid Milton
Beloved Girl
March 7, 1864–May 12, 1865

The other read:

Bethanne Sundborg Milton
Joined with her sister in heaven
before she saw a dawn
April 8, 1866

The last time she stood before a family grave was when her father died. Leah sat back against the thick trunk of the old deodar. She felt a heavy weight in her chest. What would she learn here this summer, after all?

*****

Leah pushed the heavy wood door open with one hand and hooded her nose from the rise of dust with the other. Stepping over the rough-hewn doorsill onto a crude planked wood floor, she paused to sense the quiet and dark of the abandoned log cabin. She smiled for the first time in days. She had come home.

The interior of the small cabin would not be inviting to most people, but Leah enjoyed opening the heavy blinds and letting the light come in through the small paned windows, even though most of what was revealed was dirty and dusty. She pushed open the metal latch on a small window above the kitchen sink, then took both palms and pressed the bottom pane up, releasing a spider web and letting in sweet summer air. It felt comforting, this heavy scented June, even though as she thought about the touch of breeze on her cheeks, she also felt an unwelcome and too-familiar wave of nausea.

No, she thought, *I won't let it destroy this time, too. I'm here for peace. I won't let it be a major presence in my life.*

She simply refused to die yet. She opened her purse, took out a small vial of pills and the pint of bottled water, and swallowed the blessed medicine. Leah took a deep breath and let the drug begin to take effect. She turned around, leaned back against the counter's edge, and looked at her surroundings. The kitchen was an extension of the living area, whose total floor space must be only about 12' × 20' or so. The cabinets were simple open shelves, now empty except for a few old ceramic plates and cups, and a small refrigerator hummed faintly. It and a compact four-burner gas stove, also purchased about twenty years ago when the cabin was briefly resurrected, straddled the sink counter and were bookends to a faded linoleum counter space area of about two feet in length on each side of the sink. Contemporary real estate brokers would refer to the tiny area as an "efficiency" kitchen.

She faced the length of the living area, letting the medicine move inside her. On the long wall to her left were a small river rock fireplace, the door she had come through, and one four-paned window. On her right side was a wall against which was set a small pine table with two chairs tucked underneath and a rocking chair placed to face the fireplace. On the fourth wall was a worn sofa, some lamps with faded linen shades, and a coffee table made from hand-hewn planks set on what appeared to be a couple of old wooden apple crates.

Leah recalled playing in this room as a young child, visiting Grandma one summer maybe thirty-five years ago. She remembered jumping on a big fat chair closer to the fireplace. It was gone, of course, as was her grandmother.

When she went back outside to the car, she looked again at the ramshackle cabin and remembered as a child seeing her grandmother painting the window and door sills white. Those minimal renovations were now peeling and faded, but she still loved the old place. It took four trips to cart in the linens, dishes, and utensils, along with her clothes and books, but Leah enjoyed the effort. When she finally carried her suitcases and sheets into the small bedroom and bath area behind the wall with the sofa, she was satisfied that she would be comfortable and cozy in this retreat. The mattress was aged but clean. Someone had thoughtfully aired it out recently. She would remember to call the real estate company people and thank them. She hadn't required anything of them except seeing that utilities be connected, but they had also performed this small consideration.

She took a few minutes to dust some of the more obviously dirty surfaces throughout the small home, surprised that there wasn't that much of a musty smell anywhere in the cabin. She surmised that it might be because the chinks in the logs were cracked in places and perhaps cold winter air had kept things rather fresh over the years.

Fortunately, the long Idaho summer sundown enabled Leah to finish settling in before dark, fix a quick BLT, and even have time for a hot bath in the footed porcelain tub before sleeping.

As she turned off the light on the fat pewter lamp beside her bed, Leah realized she didn't notice any remnant of her earlier nausea. That was enough to consider herself content.

*****

At first light, Leah startled out of her deep sleep. She had dreamed of her mother as a girl, running down the boardwalk of the old POP amusement park in Ocean Park. Brown short curls bobbing, Barbara wore a turquoise felt poodle skirt and matching shoes and was laughing as she hurtled past roller coasters and game booths. She carried cotton candy and a stuffed bear won in a dart throw booth.

For a moment, Leah put her hands over her eyes and let life settle in. She, Leah, was here, in this cabin, the legacy of her mother's grandmother. She opened her eyes finally to the pastel sun coming in through the high window above the aged dresser.

She tossed on her warm terry robe and fuzzy slippers and padded to the kitchen where she fixed a cup of coffee and sat with it warming her hands. She had left her purse opened on the tabletop and now took out a cellular phone and her watch. She noted the time and dialed a number in Sausalito.

"Hello?" The male voice was sleepy, and Leah looked again at her watch.

"Hi, Ned. Sorry I woke you." She could picture him, eyes still partly closed from sleep, hair ruffled, rising on an elbow to make it easier to talk.

"That's OK. How was the trip?"

"Fine."

"Is everything OK?"

"Fine. More than fine, actually. I think this is going to be perfect."

"How was the cabin? It must be a mess."

"It's perfectly adequate."

"Good. Good...is it cold there?"

"Only at night. I can always curl up in my comforter if it turns really cold. I'm fine. It's great."

"You're sure? You know you don't have to stay there, alone. You can come home. Really. If you need space, I'll just stay at the office longer. Or perhaps we can go somewhere together if the sale goes through."

Leah caught herself nodding. While part of her was irritated at his take-charge tone, she had a desire to be there for just this moment, to put her arms around his back, rest her cheek against his shoulders. Her fingers recalled the ridges of his neck.

"I know, honey, I know. But I really want to try this. No, actually, I *have* to try this. We've already had this discussion. I brought up all the literature. I'll look it over, I promise."

Ned's pause was longer than she would have wished.

"Well, anyway, I'm here. So if you change your mind, let me know. That's why you have the cell phone."

"No," Leah responded, feeling again the force of his personality, always strong, persuasive. "No. I'll call you once a week to check on everything, find out what you hear from the boys, but that's it. I don't want anyone calling me. Even you. Even though I love you. You know I love you."

"Sure, Lee." Again a pause. "Well, that's that. I've got to get ready for a big day. Oh, by the way, Fromley called yesterday and said he's coming into town next week, wants to work out the terms of the sale and so forth. So it's looking good."

"Great. I'm glad, so have a good week. If you talk to the boys, tell them I love them," Leah said, willing away a burst of vivid images of her two sons. She cradled the phone on her shoulder as she reached into her bag for their picture while she said her goodbyes, ending as always with their familiar parting words, "Be careful and safe. I love you."

She felt a rush of anguish at the photographs of Tim, now fourteen, and Jeff, twelve, taken last summer at the beach. They both resembled their father, tall and tousle-haired, broad-shouldered. Tim was experiencing a voice change and some downy brown hairs under his arms, but in that photo, he still had an early adolescent confidence. He stood with a wide stride next to the skinny, younger Jeff, whose face was softly rounded and almost girlish. They looked like the friends they were.

Leah set the frame on the table and reluctantly arose and went to the refrigerator, pulling out some yogurt and a fresh peach. She knew she mustn't let herself slip into self-recrimination over her absence. Her boys were in summer camp and thriving, and besides, this might be the last time that Tim would be interested in spending his summers in the San Juan Islands. She told herself it was the right spot for both of them. They had developed friendships with other campers while canoeing, horseback riding, sea kayaking, and generally reveling in the outdoor life of the camp.

She had already spoken with the boys once, and Ned could address any problems that arose. Yet she still felt pangs.

Why was she aching so? Perhaps it was because she had been away from them so much in the past two years. Perhaps it was just because she would miss them as any mother would when her kids went off to camp. Perhaps it was because, and it hit her with its usual fury, she was afraid that she didn't have that much time left with them and begrudged any minute she was apart.

She let the spoon of fruit rest in the bowl as she rolled these theories around. *No,* she decided. *They need a normal life. Camp is important. I mustn't feel sad in anticipation of some possible future absence...I have to see that they lead as normal a life as possible under the circumstances.* She couldn't keep them always close to her; her duty as a mother was to help nudge them from the nest. Still, she felt the hot tears slide down her cheeks. *Oh, how she missed them! She wanted everything for them, a mixed bag...security and independence, lots of love and yet self-reliance.*

As she finished her breakfast, Leah Brown ruefully concluded that a mother with hepatitis C was no less or no more neurotic than any other mother anywhere!

So when she washed up the dishes and went into the bathroom, she could stare at her face in the mirror and smile back. She didn't look bad for forty-four; she had always been told, even as a teenager, that she looked younger than she was. She took that as a compliment but always wondered how people would react to her when she got to a stage in life when she would look her age. Would she be cast into a heap and discarded like other older women?

She was a little thinner than she liked to be, much to the envy of her always-dieting friends, but at least she didn't look wan or weak. She had simply lost her appetite since she became sick. She peered closer, bending over the low sink, a sign it had been installed when people were smaller than the

11

milk-fed kin of her generation. Her brown eyes were slightly bloodshot but passable, and she had been given a straight nose, high cheekbones, and a full mouth. The word usually applied to her was "wholesome."

She finished washing her face and pulled up her long sandy-brown hair in a ponytail, went to the bedroom where she put on jeans, a denim shirt, and scruffy boots, and set out of the cabin into the hot Idaho morning. She was ready to explore.

Chapter Two

June 12, 1998

Leah paused by the edge of the creek, closer to the cabin than she had remembered. The sun was now just moving behind the trees and angled so that it no longer shone directly on her. She removed the red cotton scarf tied around her neck and bent over the wet reeds, soaking it in the icy water. Old remedy for heat, the scarf would drip cool droplets down her shoulders, between her breasts. She stood up and tied it again around her neck, then leaned down once more to cup the clear broth of the creek in her hands, splash it on her face, then let her wrists linger long enough to lower her body temperature.

Just ahead, near the bend, stood a fisherman. His back turned to her, he was thigh deep in the beaver pool, almost motionless, recalling the pose her father would assume as he contemplated his next cast. She watched him for a few moments, observing his height, the angle of his hat, a dark profile against the bright waters. If he turned back to look at her, she was sure he would be handsome, though why she couldn't imagine. Perhaps just the slope of his long back, the leanness of his form, the quiet stance, the sense that he belonged there.

Enough, she thought. *Silly woman.*

Leah arose, aware of not signaling her presence, and turned back toward home.

Chapter Three

June 16, 1998

With the late afternoon sun burning the back of her shoulders, Leah put down the garden trowel and wiped the perspiration dripping into her eyes. She felt like the biblical God after six days, ready to decree a day of rest. Somehow, those first days of her stay had flown by. She hadn't felt bored or lonely or desperate at all because she had busied herself with fixing up the primitive cabin. She had swept away cobwebs and polished the rough floors. She had put colorful towels and dishes in the kitchen. Next thing she knew, she'd be sewing happy little curtains for the cabin's five windows. She actually imagined a skylight over the kitchen but was realistic enough to figure whoever bought the place could do that.

Well, she would stop, she told herself, as soon as she tidied up the garden a bit. Years of neglect had resulted in an overgrown patch of blackberry bushes and lots of weeds, but she noted with pleasure that the berries were nearly ripe. A profusion of columbine and a healthy patch of lupines shadowed the east side of the cabin. She cleared out some of the weeds from those places, loving the *thwomp* of sound when she got the whole weed out, and then set to clearing a small sunny spot where she could put some annuals in just to make the front of the home more cheery. With the short growing season in northern Idaho, she had to choose carefully. She was almost done. She patted the rich red earth where she had planted petunias and pansies and set her tools down.

She went into the cool of the cabin, fixed a glass of iced tea, and took it outside under the shade of a thick fir tree sheltering her car. She sat in a fold-up deck chair under the bough closest to the front door and closed her eyes for a moment. Work was good. She surveyed the landscape around her. An abundance of trees enclosed the borders of the parcel of land her family still owned. At one time, other buildings had surrounded the cabin. When she had first walked the property, she had noted the barren field with shadow outlines on its perimeter and surmised that one of the structures had once been a barn. From here, she could make out the silhouette of a chimney belonging to a structure about a football field away that had been destroyed by fire. She wondered when that had been: where could she find out about it?

She thought of the life these buildings had once contained. Now only the cabin, which her mother said dated back to the 1860s, remained. Beyond the trees lay other farms, some land cleared for a housing development, the Payette River, and the town of Prospect, whose population now numbered about six thousand. The next town, a few miles south, was Miners' Rest, the county seat. Leah could barely make out any of the world beyond the trees; she felt as though she alone inhabited the area within her vision. Some echo of a time long ago still reverberated here. She loved to see the little place spring to life again.

She hadn't heard much of anything those first days except the birds. The birds! What a profusion of sound she listened to, imagining their travels and trying to identify each bird by its warble. She had brought with her a book on mountain wildflowers and one on birds of the Northwest and referred to it often to tell whether she was hearing crows, magpies, or robins. She discerned the hoots of owls in the night and noisy crows in the thicket of trees nearby. She was a novice but was relishing the quiet of her isolation and the excitement of learning these new things.

By day 3, though, she had transferred some of her Mozart CDs from the car and indulged in the joy of listening to man-made beauty. After all, she was a creature of restless habit: at home, she always had music on. She had tried to eliminate that dependency here but so far found the music soothing and good for her soul. In fact, she told herself, the music's beauty enhanced that of her surroundings. She set to wiping the walls, removing old fingerprints and occasional sticky places. At home in California, she had taken to vacuuming while accompanying the soprano in *Madame Butterfly*. Music also made chores more fun.

Filling up the quiet made it a little easier not to think about what she had come here to consider. She was feeling sufficiently good to forget for a couple of hours at a time that she had a potentially fatal disease. Now that she was almost done with feathering her nest, she'd have to stop, do some reading, and make some agonizing choices. Leah was glad that she had had these first few days of busy-ness. She would face the tough stuff soon enough.

As she sat in the folding chair, she felt a slight breeze arise from the woods and refresh her hot skin. She savored the cooling drink and leaned back in contentment. She let her mind wander.

She recalled what she could of the family history. Her pioneer great-great-grandparents had originally built the cabin sometime after the Civil War. Indeed, her middle name, Linnea, was that of her great-great-grandmother Linnea

Milton. Somewhere around the turn of the century, the little cabin ceased to be the family's primary home: they had moved into the growing town nearby. She knew her great-grandfather Esau was a lawyer there until his death from influenza in 1918. Whether out of a need to preserve family history or to hold on to an investment in land, this part of the original homestead had never been sold. Nonetheless, Esau left a sizeable inheritance to his daughter Emily, her grandmother, much of it acquired from selling off other parts of the land. What was left, about thirty acres, had remained virtually untouched for decades.

Then in the forties, Emily, widowed by the Second World War, made a trip from her California home to this remote part of Idaho to explore what was left of her heritage. Emily restored some of the original features of the neglected site and had the place fitted with modern electricity and indoor plumbing. Originally, the bathroom had been a child's bedroom. The decrepit old outhouse still leaned against a large mound of boulders at the back of the cabin.

As children, Leah's mother, Barbara, and her uncle Ed had spent a few weeks here during the summer of '47, but as Emily's responsibilities in supporting her children increased, the family didn't find the time to come back. It was only years later, after Barbara's marriage and Leah's birth in 1955, that the family began to think again about the property in Idaho. Travel was harder then without today's freeways and more dependable automobiles. Leah could remember sitting endlessly in the back seat on trips with flat tires or overheated engines the three summers they drove from Sherman Oaks to Idaho, trips that seemed to take many days and a great sense of humor to survive.

As recently as the eighties, her grandmother refurbished the appliances, but eventually, the cabin was again neglected, lying in wait until the sad reading of Emily's will reminded Leah and her mother once more of the little retreat.

Their lawyers had arranged for the sale of the acreage, but fortunately, it wasn't moving as quickly as they had originally wished. Thus, Leah found the perfect solution to her need to find a place to make her crucial decisions. It seemed especially fitting that the cabin had such a weathered and almost ageless quality about it. She sensed that the spirits inhabiting this silent corner of earth could speak to her. *Well,* she thought, *that's a bit melodramatic!* She certainly didn't believe in ghosts. But there was something that called to her in this locale, in the history around it, in the lives that were begun here. She looked forward to listening to its lessons as well as to the birds, if only she would quiet her own heart and let the messages sink in. So she decided not to lift a finger tomorrow, the seventh day of her stay here, and just open herself to the voices around her. That would be good.

Chapter Four

June 17, 1998

T he sound of light rain on the tin roof gentled Leah
awake. She stayed under the blankets for a few
moments, enjoying the change and thinking already
of the day ahead, planned only for no plans other than a trip
to the market.

Over a cup of coffee, she looked at the piles of papers she
had put out to begin reading. Since it was her seventh day,
though, she chose instead *Madame Bovary*, a book she had
always wanted to read, grabbed it and her coffee, and wrapped
her long legs under her on the old comfortable sofa. An hour
or so passed before she got up, stretched, and did some neck
exercises and yoga stretches. Her bones ached a little, a result
of the hepatitis, so she rotated her head around, then to the
left and right, working out the kinks of concentration.

She lay on her back to do a spinal twist, and as she gazed
up at the ceiling, she spotted something high above the mantel
on a deep shelf tucked into the stone recess of the fireplace. At
first, Leah thought she only imagined a glint of metal reflecting a corner of dusty sunlight, but the glimpse intrigued her.
She got up, pulled over one of the kitchen chairs, and peered
into the space, thick with dirt. She moved aside the heavy
decorative antique butter crock, which had hidden the item

from most angles of the room. She still had to stretch to reach the dark space of the shelf. Finally, by using a broom handle from the fireplace and iron tools, she inched the corner of the metal thing toward her. It was a box, approximately five inches deep and measuring about ten inches wide and twelve inches long.

Sneezing from the riot of dust, she took the box down to the kitchen counter and rattled it, finding that it contained one heavy object that shifted slightly inside. She wiped the rusted lock with a paper towel, but it refused to come apart.

A few minutes later, silently thanking Ned for his foresight in outfitting the car trunk, she let the light rain wet her while she searched the contents of the kit meant to change tires. It held a few other miscellaneous tools as well. Leah took them in and tried several, shaking her sore hands, until one pried the lock apart.

When she took off the tightly sealed lid, Leah discovered a book with a heavy black leather cover. She carefully extracted it, washed her hands, poured herself another cup of coffee, and opened the cover. Inside, on a frontispiece of faded silk moiré, an elegant hand proclaimed this diary to be the property of Linnea Milton. Trembling now, Leah realized she had the diary of her great-great-grandmother, the first of her family to have settled in the West and reside in this home. She turned the page and saw Linnea's immaculate script filling each page of parchment.

Leah looked at the first lines, the original black India ink applied with a quill pen and faded to a drab but nonetheless discernible brown. The entry said,

April 8, 1863
I begin this diary today at the start of a new life. I, Linnea Sundborg Milton, the wife of Thaddeus Horatio Milton, am

embarking today from Independence, Missouri, on what very well may be a perilous journey out West. It is strange to think that we are actually beginning a journey that Thaddeus has been planning for so many months. He has longed to leave the East ever since his brother Jacob died in Virginia fighting the Confederates. His hopes to homestead somewhere in the territories burn more brightly today than ever. Besides, he says, there is no slavery in Oregon Territory.

I hope it does not diminish his fervor to say that I do not share his pleasure at this prospect. I hope God will forgive me for writing that I am thus disposed due to the pain of leaving my family. Already, in the few weeks since we left Boston, I miss them. I can picture my parents reading by the fire in our home and my brother Samuel playing with his strange inventions. He is always building something! I wish I could speak with them now, perhaps even join my mother to hold her yarn while she rolls it into balls. I used to hate that chore, but now I would truly enjoy it.

I yearn most especially for my sister, as we have shared our laughter and secret thoughts since we could first speak. Ingrid is only a year older than I am, and I do not know what I will do without her. We have spent almost every minute of our lives together, walking to the school at the edge of the neighborhood, making each other laugh at silly things, reading passages together when we find an exciting book, learning how to quilt, and talking about our dreams. Ingrid wants to be as good a cook as Mother, and I planned to be a teacher, like my favorite person, Miss Theodosia Perkins, my teacher when I was thirteen. She read to us with the most expressive and firm voice. Even cleaning up after dinner was fun with Ingrid at my side.

In spite of that loss, however, I love and respect Mr. Milton and so will faithfully honor our marriage vows and accompany him to the farthest corners of the earth if necessary.

We have read many treatises about life out West, some of the accounts frightening and some most promising. Whatever befalls us I will record in this journal so that there may be a chronicle of our lives for my family. I must also admit that I feel already some strength through simply writing down my thoughts in this manner. Perhaps God has devised a way for me to better accept my fate. I may not be able to speak with Ingrid, but I can talk through these pages.

We are leaving in the morning with thirty-five other wagons. I trust that our wagon master, who is very experienced, will help us in this daunting task.

P.S. I do not intend this as a daily diary, as the passage through these territories is arduous and may not provide me time for what may be a frivolity.

*****

Leah noted the rejoinder and identified with the young woman who believed in the concept of a daily diary. She remembered when, as a twelve-year-old, she had been given a diary at Christmas and began it with a New Years' Day entry, "Today my pajamas froze on the line." That detail may have noted an unusual occurrence for San Rafael, California, but the language was not especially provocative! The remaining ten or so entries were also perfunctory, the required daily writing reflecting the routine of junior high life rather than any depth of perception. After ten days, she had abandoned the effort, feeling guilty at not somehow writing clever observations. Only as an adult did Leah understand that journals could be used for recording inner thoughts, not for the dull reporting of daily trivia in some misguided effort to do justice to a daily diary.

Before reading the next entry, dated nine days later, Leah violated her promise not to use the cell phone and dialed her mother's number in San Rafael.

After five rings, her mother answered.

"Hi, Mom?"

"Hi, dear. Are you all right? I wasn't expecting to hear from you. Is everything OK?"

"Sure," Leah said, biting her lip at the rush of unexpected tears. Her voice caught. "I'm fine. I'm sorry. I didn't mean to frighten you." She grabbed a tissue. "I mean, after I made all that fuss about not being in touch while I'm here."

"Of course, dear," said her mother. "Tell me what's so important."

"I don't know where to start. Except to say that this is a special little place." She listened for a moment to her mother's breath. "The most amazing thing happened. I found something today, way up high, tucked on a shelf off the beam by the fireplace."

"Yes?"

"It's your great-grandmother's diary. Grandmother Linnea's. Have you read it?"

There was an audible sigh on the line. "No, dear. I never heard of it. Wish I had!"

"Well," said Leah, her excitement rising, "It does look like no one's read it for eons. It was in an airtight metal box, almost entirely hidden from view." She patted the book, closed on her lap. "I'm wondering who the last person to have opened it was! Probably Grandmother. Anyway, I'm going to read it. I'll bring it home with me. I just thought maybe you knew about it."

They chatted for a few minutes about other things. Her mother had received postcards from the boys, and in spite of the usual camp adjustments, all seemed well. When Leah hung up the phone, she realized it had been almost a week since she had spoken to Ned.

Nonetheless, she decided to phone him later in the day. Right now, she needed to get outside and walk, try to put at ease her thundering heart, resisting the impulse to read more of the diary just now.

She put on her hiking boots, wrapped a light jacket around her waist, grabbed her fanny pack and some snacks from the refrigerator, and headed for the trails near the river.

She felt the breaths of ghosts on the back of her neck.

Chapter Five

So here she was, atop an aspen-crowded hill overlooking the small town below, almost gasping for breath from her climb. She enjoyed a long drink from her water bottle, appreciating the fanny pack which held two containers. She sat down against a stray log, took out the tangerine she had grabbed before leaving the cabin, and stilled herself for a few minutes while she enjoyed the simple ritual of peeling the soft fruit; its fat segments promised sweet juice. Each shedding of the rind was a tangible joy to Leah. The sicker she got, the more she appreciated these small pleasures, it seemed. The bite of tangerine taste here on a hill in hot summertime was not to be underrated. Leah used her sleeve to wipe off the splash of juice that had dribbled on her chin and hunched forward, placing the rinds in the fanny pack. She bent her knees, placing her elbows on her thighs, cupping her chin in her hands. She gazed at the panorama before her.

On the east side of the river, the valley below was crowded with a main street, cars, and tiny figures. She wasn't more than a mile away from the center of town, but she could feel as removed from its bustle as if it didn't exist. She could picture the streets below her once covered with wild grasses and devoid of human activity. What must it have been like to be her great-great-grandmother and, after a long day, perhaps, pull into that narrow valley below with the wagons? Maybe she hadn't even known that this was where they would settle. How much did one valley look like another? How many times must she have longed to stay in a place of green rivers only to move on the next day? How tired she must have been!

She moved away from the log, lay back on the firm earth, and gazed at the sky. She remembered the long California afternoons of her childhood, when she and Jeanette, her best friend in the second grade, would climb the hill behind her Sherman Oaks home late in the afternoons. Knowing they would soon have to suspend their world of dolls and bicycles and building forts to return home for dinner, they would lie back just as she was doing now, heads cradled under crossed hands, their bony knees emerging under the cuffs of their dark blue denim pedal pushers. Looking at the march of white fluff in the blue sky above, she and Jeanette would talk about the clouds, about Carl Sandburg's *Rootabaga Stories* and his imagined world in the sky, the possibility of marshmallow stepping-stones to the heavens. They'd chew on the thin and juicy weeds that lined their favorite spot, feeling nearly grown-up in their control of their own tiny universe, one of pussy willows and poppies, scratchy brush underneath their sweaters, and the sun tingling their foreheads.

Jeannette and she had promised to be best friends always. When they built dollhouses out of orange crates, they pretended they were next-door neighbors; their wee doll-people traded babysitting and recipes as their own parents did. They were young, and in 1963, embraced by the arms of the earth on a mellow July afternoon, all things seemed possible.

Only soon after, Leah recalled, her world changed forever. It was all linked to the president's assassination, somehow. Summer was over and she was in school on a chilly late November morning when the principal called an emergency assembly and announced that President Kennedy had been shot and lay dead in Dallas. And then there was that whole weekend of watching Caroline and John-John and their beautiful mother and sharing the whole country's mourning. Even that Sunday with the big black-and-white television on all the time, they watched, as over her Cheerios, Lee Harvey Oswald was shot.

It all seemed to start that weekend—though as a grownup she knew better—her parents' stony silence at the dinner table, her mother's red eyes, the cold glasses with the smell of vodka and remnants of olives that her mother thought she had hidden, the absence of her father more and more, and then the final announcement: a move to Northern California in June and how Daddy would stay in LA "just until we get settled." But Daddy stayed there forever. Their home became just little Davey and Leah and Mama at work instead of at home for cookies and milk after school: no more Jeanette, no more wobbly bike rides up and down Ventura Canyon Road, no more hot San Fernando Valley summers, a life gone, shot out from her as was JFK from his world.

She and Jeanette wrote each other for a while, letters filled with "I miss you's" and plans for visits. But Mother didn't really like the trips back home to LA, and when Grandma Emily moved from Santa Monica up to Mill Valley so she could be closer to them, well, there seemed little reason to make the ten-hour drive to see old friends. How many times, Leah reflected, had she written "See you soon!" on letters to Jeannette and other friends only to find that somehow losing touch was the norm. Everyone moved, got new jobs, transferred up, and misplaced addresses. She hoped Jeanette was happy now somewhere in the world, which had changed so much since their short time together.

As clearly as if the orange crate houses were in front of her now, Leah could picture the tiny doll foursome she had collected: a mother with apron, father with perfectly slick brown hair, and two children, a boy and a girl. Her miniature family sat at a wee mahogany table and, in her childish imagination, talked of happy days together: early models of family behavior! As her own mother and father parted, and so many of her friends' parents shifted with the mores of the sixties, she wondered what little girls did today with their Barbies and fantasy dolls. Did four perfect little people still sit down as a nuclear family at the dinner table together?

She watched the same sky now as she had with her young friend and lingered under its beneficence a while longer before she rose and began the rest of her journey to the market.

The sun was getting lower, as Leah reflected on the beauty of this day, on the flood of her memories. She picked up a smooth stone from the spot where she had just rested and put it in her pocket. She would add it to her collection of stones. Standing up, she moved the rock to her fanny pack, stretched her arms up to the far blue, and thanked God or perhaps her mother's AA Higher Power, for the strength to delight in another day.

When she came home and rested on the sofa, she opened the diary and devoured the rest of it, staying up most of the night to finish.

*****

April 17, 1863
This has been the first time I dare to add to my diary. We have traveled many miles during this beginning of our journey,

but I fear that we haven't been able to cover as great a distance as Thaddeus had intended. It seems we have traveled only about a hundred miles. All seemed hopeful when we began our travels. We had cold but sunny weather for the first two days, a good omen, as it allowed us to share buoyant spirits with each other. One family, especially, seems like ours in values and expectations. The Smiths, Helen, Josiah, and their infant girl, Amanda, are most friendly. We met in Independence and discovered that we grew up only a few miles from each other back in Boston, so there is a kinship already. Helen and I even read the same books in school! They arrived here by stagecoach two days earlier than we did. Our trip began as theirs, by coach, but we went a different route and took a steamboat to gather at the Missouri River for the last part of the trip.

Unfortunately, after our first two days on the wagon train, heavy rains have plagued us most of the way and many days our wagons have been mired in mud. Thaddeus and Josiah have become closer friends due to the times they have had to help each other pull our wagons out of the slippery mud.

I must admit that I had a different vision of what this trip would be like. We are isolated most of the day from the conversation of others, as the women walk with their own wagons and then are busy helping with chores and the preparation of food whenever we stop. At night, we are all so tired from the incessant bumping along and the beating of rain that we retire early to our beds.

I hope to know Helen better as the sunshine returns, and we can even see each other from our wagons! I miss my dear Ingrid terribly. One thing we always shared, and I hesitate to write this down, was that when it was our time of the month we could tell each other. I am experiencing that now, with very severe stomach cramps, but I feel unable to discuss this with anyone. So, dear diary, you will have to be the place I tell of my frustration with *the mess of this curse and the discomfort as we bounce along. I do not feel any privacy left for me.*

I remind myself that God gave women this monthly devastation so they could bear children, but I must say that it may have been easier on women who lived simpler lives. We are so encumbered by heavy clothes and now wet layers of covers! I must remember to hold little Amanda Smith so I can remind myself of the reason for these feminine troubles. Perhaps someday I, too, shall be blessed with a beautiful infant. I know how much that would please Thaddeus.

As I retire tonight, I will pray to God for the strength I know I possess to continue this trust I have in my dear husband. He is, of course, right in his desire to homestead.

Yes, he is!

*****

June 22, 1998

Dear Tim and Jeff:

I talked with Grandma and she read me your postcards. Thank you so much for sending them. I'm happy that you are doing well. Tim, I think that the responsibility of feeding the camp horses is a sign of good things for you. It means that they consider you a strong and mature member of the camp community. Maybe you will be interested in being a counselor one of these days! At any rate, I am proud of you and that you are considered so trustworthy!

And, Jeff, I understand that you are a bit upset by not being in your brother's cabin, but have you thought that you now have a chance to make some new friends? Pretty soon, Tim will be too old to continue in camp anyway, and I think it is wonderful that you are now old enough to be more on your own.

Now that I am here in the family cabin, I can't believe that we haven't come here all of your lives. It is very tiny, but it is in a beautiful spot, not far from the river and a forest of trees. I almost feel like I am at summer camp, too. I went fly fishing the other day. I will tell you all about it when I see you again—no fish stories in this letter—but I plan to explore the creek more tomorrow and maybe catch (and release) something this time!

I am really resting and thinking a lot about both of you. I found a wonderful diary written by my great-great-grandmother, Linnea, who lived in this very cabin in the 1860s. She didn't have the things I do here now, like indoor plumbing and a refrigerator, but I can still really imagine what it may have been like to live here so long ago. Can you believe that she actually came here in a covered wagon?

I am trying not to use my car or phone very much, and I think I shall walk into town tomorrow to mail this.

I can't wait to share this with you and to give you both big hugs (OK, not in public.) I love you like the tollhouse cookies Momma made!

XOXO, Mom

Chapter Six

June 23, 1998

The post office in Prospect was really only about two miles from the cabin. As she dropped the letter to the boys in the mail, Leah stood for a moment, relishing the absence of pain: she hadn't paused at any time on her walk. Perhaps this was a sign that she could proceed on the next step of her attempts to stall hepatitis without again undergoing Interferon. She promised herself to read some of the papers she had carried with her as soon as she returned to the cabin. It was time to settle down for that part of her time up here. In congratulation, she treated herself to a low-fat ice cream cone.

She licked the sweet chocolate ripples in the coffee ice cream as she always had, with slow circular motions, pushing the vanishing ice cream into smaller peaks with each lick, leaving little trace of the ice cream in the cone before she finished that off. As she strolled down the streets of the town, she occasionally glimpsed herself in a window, thinking that what she saw reflected somehow the adolescent within her adult frame. Was it the ice cream cone or being in a place that reminded her of summer camp? Whatever the reason, she felt remarkably vibrant and youthful, almost carefree.

Leah paused by the real estate office that had listed the cabin for sale. The small white clapboard structure had gained additions but still kept the flavor of its origins, indicated by the sign "Founded 1935." It featured a wrap-around porch on three sides, with inviting wicker chairs. In the two large bay windows on either side of the entry were advertisements indicative of burgeoning prosperity. Pictures of tidy cottages, the same vintage as the office, accompanied glowing descriptions: "Ranchette for sale. Must see! 2 bedroom, 1 bath cozy cottage sitting pretty on 40 acres, barn and outbuildings included. Estate sale. $400,000." Another urged the buyer to consider "Hideaway: private yet close to town. Immaculate first home, adjacent to US Forest Service land. Seller motivated. Make offer!" Her cabin wasn't featured. Fine with her.

She remembered that she had intended to thank those responsible for the preparation of the cabin, and so, wiping her sticky hands on her jeans, she opened the door and passed into the chilly air-conditioned offices.

A young woman with a retro Farrah Fawcett hairdo looked up. She finished writing a sentence and then turned her attention to Leah.

"May I help you?"

"Thank you. I'm Leah Brown. I'm staying out at my family's cabin, the Milton place, and I wanted to talk to the person who arranged the cleaning and stuff for me." Leah was aware of someone looking at her from the bench near the entry door.

"Oh. Sure. Is there a problem?"

"No. I feel stupid, but I can't remember the woman's name. I just wanted to thank her. I was in town and stopped by on impulse."

As usual, Leah sensed that she was giving more information than she needed to. Her sons were always rolling their eyes when they ate out and Leah felt compelled to tell her waitress that she was on a diet, as though she needed a rationale to order a small portion.

"Hold on a minute," the girl said, as she rifled through a file box on her desk. "That would be Betty Andreason. It's her listing. She's not in at the moment, but I'll be glad to give her a message."

"Oh. Thanks. I feel silly, of course I remember her now. Well," Leah said, "If you could just tell her that I stopped by to let her know how much I appreciate the job she did. I'm having a wonderful time. The cabin is adorable. I love the mountains. Oh, but then you probably don't need to know all that. Anyway, thanks."

Leah turned around to leave and tripped on a boot belonging to the stranger she'd glimpsed out of the corner of her eye. She felt so clumsy.

"Whoops. I'm sorry!" she said, as she caught herself before falling by extending a hand to the wall.

"No. Please, *I'm* sorry," the stranger said. "I don't know why I had to be in such a sprawl! Please excuse me."

Leah turned her attention to him. He was about her age, perhaps a bit younger, but looked much more like he belonged in this part of the country than she did. Actually, he reminded her of the fishing figure she'd seen the other day. His boots were worn, his jeans faded in all the right places to just the shade a city kid would envy, and he even held a Stetson hat in his lap. He smiled at her and offered his hand.

She took his hand and noticed that it was rough and callused. He must be a working man, she thought.

"Oh, that's all right. I don't know why I didn't look more carefully. Anyway, thanks. I'm fine." She removed her hand from his and backed away, aware of his gaze.

"I'm Adam Caldwell," the man said, as he arose. She noticed his height, probably around 6'4". "I know about your cabin, the Milton cabin."

Leah found herself upset by the news.

"Oh," she said. "You mean you've looked at my place?"

"Not yet, but I was going to mention it along with some other cabins I've seen signs on."

Of course. There was a For Sale sign out by the end of her driveway. Why was she feeling irritable about it?

"So, Ms. Brown," he continued. "I may just be by."

"It's *Mrs.* Brown. And how do you know my name?" Leah asked, more uncomfortable with each exchange of words.

"I heard you introduce yourself to the receptionist. This is a pretty tiny office, as you just realized." He glanced down at his boots.

"Of course. Well," Leah heard herself using "well" to pause again, to buy time, "I'd better be going. Nice to meet you, Mr. Caldwell."

Leah somehow wanted him to know that she remembered his name too. She wanted to ask him if he fished.

She left, feeling as awkward as a thirteen-year-old in her gym shorts.

All the way home, she reflected on her brief encounter with this man. Why did he matter? When she reached the cabin, her cell phone was ringing. Ned. She remembered that she was supposed to have called him yesterday. How could she be so careless?

"Hello?" Leah put down the house keys and sat in the small kitchen chair.

"Darling? It's Ned. Are you all right? I started to worry when I didn't hear from you yesterday." His deep voice was edged with annoyance, but it was slight enough that if she challenged him, he would convince her that she was exaggerating.

"No, I'm fine, really. I spent a long day out on a hike yesterday and wrote the boys after dinner. I guess the time just passed, and I forgot. I'm sorry."

She could picture him leaning back in his swivel chair, gazing out at Alcatraz while they spoke. She wondered if it was a clear day, how the sun was glancing off the white caps of the Bay. She imagined him restless with irritation, a tense figure against the serene view of water.

"You know, Leah, we agreed that I wouldn't call you. But the deal was that you would call me every week. I've been waiting."

"Again, I'm sorry, I'm sorry, I'm sorry! What else can I say? Damn it!"

Leah bit her lip. Why was she so angry that he was calling her on her failure to live up to the deal they'd made? She grabbed a pencil and started to doodle a triangle. She told herself to calm down.

"My, my…must've pushed a button. You can't really be mad at me for wanting to know what's going on. I talked to the boys yesterday and couldn't wait to share it with you when you called, that's all. Why are you so touchy?" Now his anger was no longer disguised.

"I…I don't really know, Ned. I've just been enjoying the peace and quiet of my new little life here. I like the absence of negatives, to be truthful."

Now she felt the heat rising in her chest. She hated confrontations. She picked up a red marker and added concentric circles to the triangle

"Peace and quiet? Is talking to your husband, the husband who loves you—and who gave you this freedom to be alone, by the way—is that really such an intrusion?"

Now Ned realized he was sounding martyred, but he had some issues to settle.

At his strong voice, Leah felt her defenses fading. The truth was, she had been resenting him for always being there, for his hovering over her, even when she knew she would have blamed him for being less supportive. This damned illness had screwed up more than her body. She began filling in the lines between the circles.

"Look," she said, "let's not fight. I'm sorry I let the date slip. You know I love you and appreciate all you've done. I just *need* to do this."

"You mean by 'do this' that you need to think about us?"

The conversation was taking another bad turn.

"No, I didn't mean that." Leah realized with a shock that she *did* mean that. She put down the pencil, pushed back her chair, reached behind her to the sink, and grabbed a pear from the bowl of fruit. She waited for more from Ned before she continued but gave up after a few seconds.

"No…I meant about the illness. You know we've been through it all before I'm not rejecting you by needing to be away. And by the way, you didn't give me the right to do this." Her pitch was rising. "It wasn't a *gift* from you. I'm a grown woman who has every right to do what I can to heal myself and to feel good about my decisions. I'm not your servant, to be allowed or permitted to do things at your beck and call."

She knew she sounded like a fiery woman's libber, but it was true that she felt her back tingle when he was condescending. She bit into the savory pear.

"I don't know how to respond to this sudden hostility from you, Leah. I'm going to hang up and wait for you to call me when you have things in better perspective." Ned paused to allow his words to sink in. "So unless you have something else you're burning to say, I'll just hear from you when I hear from you. Bye, then."

Leah heard the click of the receiver before she caught her breath long enough to respond. Where was the rest of the usual goodbye? She arose from the table, put the half-eaten pear into the sink, and leaned over the rough edge of the counter. She felt sick. She hadn't asked for more news about the boys. She hadn't even asked about John Fromley, the pending sale, anything. What was she doing?

Chapter Seven

May 21, 1863

I *can hardly bear to write of the events of this day. Yesterday, Helen Smith was attacked by diarrhea and, as we needed to forge ahead, tried valiantly not to tell the wagon master. But yesterday afternoon, as we stopped for some water for the oxen, she began to vomit most violently. When I finally persuaded her to rest, she felt very hot, and I knew she had a high fever. We have heard stories of the many people who have died on their passage to the West but felt that we had somehow been blessed by escaping the scourge of illness that others recounted.*

Last week, we met some other overlanders returning to the East. They told us that their caravan had been afflicted by the cholera to such an extent that almost half of them had died, so they were not going to try to go any further. No promise of riches at the end of the trail could persuade them to continue.

Now I wonder if they had not been infected with the disease and spread it to us!

***

June 25, 1998

Leah had left the small bedroom window open to allow in the frosty Idaho night. Now, as she turned over to adjust the angle of her pillow, she felt the icy blast tickle her nose. The diary lay opened on her lap. She glanced at her travel alarm and noted it was 3:30 a.m. Simultaneously, she was possessed of a violent fear, an unreasonable intrusion on whatever she had found peaceful in her dreams.

A childhood prayer ran through her mind, "If I should die before I wake..." and then she realized what was in her subconscious. She didn't want to die. She felt a physical wrenching in her stomach as she thought of not being, of vanishing from this earth. No more smelling the scented air, no more warmth of the down comforter, no more cabin, no more eyesight, no more body. The thoughts were almost palpable. No, no, no. How could she imagine it all being over, the reality of her existence on earth?

She wished now she had the easy palliatives of her childhood faith, wished now that she could truly believe in an afterlife, in the passage of her soul to some other plane of existence. But here in this still country night, she couldn't call up the belief. She could only imagine losing her sense of self.

And then she tried deliberately to put the unbidden thoughts away with the mantra that wasting precious time in life worrying about death was futile. She told herself all the things she had listed before to wipe away the clench of pain: *think about beauty, think about love, think about Ned and your children, think about what joy there is in life now, today.* She added, *Tonight, even at 3:30 a.m. Just be glad you're here and don't spend even a moment of your time on earth fearing what all human beings have to face. When it comes, that will be enough time to face it.*

Stop, stop, stop!

Eventually, Leah's beating heart quieted, and she turned on the light. There wasn't any reason she couldn't just get up now. She had no schedule, except for fishing sometime early in the morning. And even that wasn't required. For the first time in many years no one needed her. Her boys were safe; Ned was somewhere deep in his always-untroubled sleep. Even after their argument last night, she knew he would read for a few minutes, then turn out the bedside light and fall into a sound sleep, totally untroubled by whatever had happened during the day. Her family's maxim of settling fights before saying goodnight didn't seem necessary to Ned. He dispensed with all that superstitious nonsense, as he put it, cleared out his thoughts, and easily renewed himself by a solid sleep.

She remembered the first time they had ever made love: afterward, Leah had turned to Ned's strong back, put her arms around him, and whispered, "That was wonderful, Ned."

She heard no response, lifted herself up to lean over his broad shoulders, and peek at his face. He was asleep, must have been so almost immediately after they finished.

At that time, young and wildly in love, Leah had thought perhaps his sleep was due to the rigors of the day they had spent sailing in San Francisco Bay. The wind had been lively and their small skiff had bobbed ferociously all afternoon. Ned had enjoyed wearing his captain's hat, keeping the boat on course and teaching Leah a few things about the art of sailing. She had admitted to feeling bone-tired until they began to make love. Then all her energy was focused on the delights of being with this one person, of feeling so acutely his kisses, of the parting of her lips, and then of herself as she welcomed him.

Over the years since, Leah had discovered that the deep sleep she had seen that first night was not due to the exhaustion of passion but simply to some trigger inside her mate. No matter what had happened at work or between them or even with fear about some prospect ahead, Ned slept quickly and well.

She wasn't going to go back to sleep, she knew, so she threw the covers aside, put on her robe and slippers, and padded to the kitchen. Her daily assortment of medications was lined up on the sink, but she ignored them and boiled water for tea.

When she crawled back into bed with Earl Gray warming her hands, she opened Linnea's diary to the passage she had begun last night. She had now re-read several pages and had been surprised at how much the archaic language had nonetheless communicated the life of that woman and that time. They were at the end of the caravan's sixth week of passage. The early references to personal and feminine concerns had been eclipsed by Linnea's attempts to depict the daily life of her family and new acquaintances. Leah had read about the drudgery of the trip and marveled at the time it took to travel even a few miles: they had spent nearly five weeks and covered less than five hundred miles. It was now late May, and the caravan had already lost two wagons. Some of the disasters had been chronicled: the death of oxen, the illness of friends, and the difficulties caused by weather, especially the slow progress made when the prairie winds blew black heavy currents of thick dust to block their passage.

This entry, however, reached out directly to Leah.

May 22, 1863

By this morning, my dear Helen was burning with such a fever that she was unaware of the rest of the world around her. As I held her head in my lap, I tried to think of things I could do to help, but no matter how many cold cloths I pressed on her forehead, no matter how many times I entreated her to keep up her courage, no matter how many times my tears mixed with the drops of perspiration on her brow, she just continued to burn. It was as though her skin had dried up like parchment, and as the morning wore on, it seemed to tighten over her cheekbones, leaving the sense of dust on my fingertips. At noon, she began convulsing, and by the time the other women in camp were washing the dishes from lunch, she was gone. She looked up into the sky with her eyes fixed on something very far away, shuddered, and gave up the ghost. As her spirit left her, I recalled her telling me once that she would soon observe her nineteenth birthday.

We have buried her next to another fresh gravestone near our camp, that of a stranger also taken by this illness. Her husband is sorely grieved and has asked me to care for Amanda during the rest of the journey. I do so with a heavy burden of sadness in my heart. Helen and I both hoped we could settle near each other. She has been the one person in whom I could confide my fears and hopes. Now she is gone, as are her plans for a new life. I will care lovingly for sweet Amanda and pray for Helen's soul, but I must confess here that my hopes have been dashed. Of course, I am determined to continue to be a helpmate to Thaddeus and to support his plans, but at this juncture I do wish we had never left the comforts of our families.

*****

Leah set down the journal, closed her eyes, and let the images of that distant day sink in. As always, she searched for the sub-text of the diary, all the things which even Linnea in her secret candor could still not write. She imagined Leah thinking but not daring to commit to paper, "I hate this journey. I never asked to be a pioneer." How much of a diary reflects the actual truth of experience?

If she were to record her feelings, for instance, about her argument with Ned last night, would she dare to note every single emotion that she had experienced? Would she have recorded her irritation at Ned's really most natural reaction? Would she have wanted him to know that just for a moment yesterday, she had felt feminine and attractive again at the acknowledgement of a new man's glance? How long had it been since she and Ned had paid attention to the love life they had enjoyed for so many years? How had their preoccupation with her illness dampened their erotic life?

She felt perspiration on her brow and something like a hot flash burn her cheeks, so she got out of bed and opened the high window a crack. A rush of sweet and crisp night air came in, carrying smells of pine and fir.

Back in bed, the reality of her situation was evident. She felt sick with pain and a sudden and unwelcome sense of chagrin. Her unkind thoughts about Ned, the odor of summer trees, the icy air, and the feeling of being on an island remote from what she really needed assailed her, and Leah remembered why. Camping. The cold night above her tent and sleeping bag. The trip last summer with the boys, the trip that Ned had planned to take her away from her unhappy routine.

She had been near the end of her treatments but still suffering terribly from wracking bone aches and nausea. In between injections, she would feel a little better, but still was worn out and in great discomfort. She had tried to explain to Ned that it was akin to having the flu every day but not knowing that it would ever end.

Poor Ned, in trying to fix things, had planned, unbeknownst to her, a weekend family trip to a campsite near Lake Tahoe. He had brought the boys into their bedroom one Friday afternoon during one of those brief respites between injections. She lay on top of the bed. His voice, bright, cheery, and oh-so-optimistic, still echoed.

"Lee, get dressed. The boys and I have a surprise. We're all ready, and you don't have to do a thing."

She looked at the three of them smiling at her and kept quiet. As she got up and added shoes and a sweater to her usual tee shirt and sweatpants outfit, Ned kept chattering as though to stave off any objections she might have. The boys occasionally chimed in.

"You'll see, honey. A change of scenery will do wonders. It's been so long since we've been anywhere as a family. It'll be wonderful. Like old times."

So reluctantly, she found herself bundled up in the front seat of the Jeep, with boys and talk and music and excitement filling the car. She felt lousy all the way to the lake, tried not to cry when evening fell and she lacked the energy to walk down to the water with the three of them.

Even the next morning, as Ned valiantly made breakfast in the frosty breeze, she yearned to be home in her own bed. She spent the whole Saturday in a camp chair, watching her family swim and cook and play and have fun in spite of her.

At one time during the afternoon, Jeff ran back from the lake, his brown smooth shoulders beaded with water, his hair dripping in his eyes. His smile was huge. As he approached, she wanted to jump up and hug him and embrace this perfect moment for her family, but felt too weak to stir. She loved them so much. She felt like an outsider.

When Jeff asked her how she was doing, she said, "Oh, honey. Fine. I'm just fine."

He smiled and turned back to the water. *Fine.* How many times she had spoken those words, denying how she really felt?

She was ashamed that she resented the whole trip, the way it had been sprung on her, and hated most of all her self-loathing at what she perceived as giving into the discomfort, not being a good sport, wanting to be anywhere but where she was. She couldn't stand whiners, and she had become one.

Ned had meant well, but all it did was increase her sense of martyrdom and disquiet, then overwhelm her with remorse that she wasn't appreciating his efforts. That night, when he came to share the double sleeping bag they'd bought as honeymooners, she stiffened at his touch. She wanted to be able to thank him for the work he had done, to give him a warm hug. She knew on an intellectual plane that he was doing the best he could, putting duct tape on the problems, fixing things in his own way, but she couldn't even say that. Instead, before she had time to censor herself, she had turned toward him and hissed, "I just wish you could feel like I do for only one day. Then you'd know what it was like."

Ned, struck silent by the fury of her words, fell asleep anyway. She had stayed awake until the fluorescent dial on her watch said 4:30 a.m., ashamed of herself and feeling petty and ungrateful yet hating Ned for putting her in this position.

She knew now that one of the side effects of any serious illness was how it affected a marriage and other family relations in strange ways unknown to those who hadn't experienced it. She also knew this was a strong reason she had come to the cabin. She needed to learn how to deal with those who also were victimized by her disease. Mr. Fixit (her new and unspoken nickname for Ned) wasn't at fault. He was damned if he did and damned if he didn't. She felt helpless to deal with this turn in their relationship. Why had she resented his taking control of the very things she at the same time felt relieved no longer to deal with: the household finances, many decisions about the boys, even planning for dinner? She had felt too exhausted to take care of so many things, especially when she had undergone the Interferon treatment, but then she didn't like the feeling of dependence she had had to develop.

Either she had to accept this more graciously or leave. There didn't seem to be any other answer. So poor Ned, indeed! Would he want to read about all of this, to see himself portrayed with such venom? And what did her ingratitude say about her own character flaws?

Now as she envisioned Helen's burial on a wind-swept plain with the Rockies in distant view, Leah acknowledged Linnea's courage in writing what she had. But with a woman's instinct, Leah knew there was much left unwritten. What about Thaddeus? Linnea's cursory reminders of her wifely duty never mentioned their intimate life. Leah wondered if Thaddeus had been a considerate lover—indeed, whether that was even an expectation of Linnea's generation. If not, how had Linnea dealt with the requirements of womanhood? There had been an embarrassed mention of menstruation, but what about all the other things? How did people make love with other wagons so near, with the lack of privacy? Did women in the 1860s talk of such things, even in the quiet of rare moments together? Had Thaddeus even thought about such efforts as washing sheets after love-making? Did he, too, fall into deep sleep when Linnea may have wished a tender caress? How could diaries of that time have recorded the truth of women's lives?

Chapter Eight

June 10, 1863

We are at last at Fort Larami, some 640 miles from our Missouri beginnings. Amanda is taking a nap, and I have time to record my thoughts. Although we have had a fairly successful crossing, I am discouraged to be reminded that we have traversed only about one-third of the way. Looking back on the events of these past several weeks, I must say that we did experience some remarkably good fortune, as the Indians we encountered were friendly. After trading some materials with our wagon leader, Mr. Price, they left us alone. At home, I had read about the massacres of 1854 near Fort Boise and was afraid of the Cheyennes and the Sioux, but I am heartened that what I envisioned has not occurred. Even the gobacks we've met have not experienced Indian hostilities; instead, they've been vanquished by homesickness or cholera or loss of wagons or sick oxen.

The hot winds have been irritating, but our oxen have survived. I feared for our safety the most when several wagons overturned where the Missouri and Platte Rivers come together, and along with losing many material possessions, we lost some of the oxen. We are very dependent on forces outside of our control, and I am learning lessons about having to accept some of the more dire consequences of our pioneer spirit!

I also have to remember that even a non-adventurous life can often be fraught with danger: certainly the hostilities we were experiencing with the War Between the States created a great fear even at home. There was little security there, either. Had Thaddeus not had a limp from his childhood accident, he may well have served in the Union forces. I might have lost him then. At least we are choosing the rugged trials we are enduring for the promise of a better life.

I believe we have benefited from being latecomers to the passage. Thousands of people have preceded us. They have left excellent accounts telling of places to find water and of places to avoid. We have good trail maps and even find posted notes on the trail for us as we travel. It's what we call the Prairie Post Office. Sometimes, the messages are left on trees or rocks or even on human skulls. (These Mr. Price refers to as the Bone Express.) Yesterday at a bend in the road, there was a large rock on which someone had painted a warning, "Do not drink from this stream. The waters is poisoned."

I admit to being very tired, aware of the added respon-sibilities of taking care of my little charge, Amanda. I believe she misses the milk from her mother's breast and finds what we give her pale comfort. I also sorely miss her mother. Although we had to bury five more people who have died since Helen, I am grateful that only a few others of our party got the contagion. Thus far, I have escaped any severe illness and count myself fortunate. I am sustained by the smiles of sweet Amanda, the courage and hard work of my husband, and the pride I feel at being his helpmeet.

Today, I will have an opportunity to wash out our clothes and blankets and sheets here in the rest time of the Fort. We have planned to stay two days and are invited tonight to a dinner and party with song and dance. The men are engaged in trading and purchasing supplies for the next part of our journey through the pass.

My only wish now would be that I could talk with Ingrid, though even she—and this record—cannot share my most secret thoughts, expressed only in my mind. I have posted a letter to her; one of the officers at the Fort says he will see that it gets sent back to Boston. I can say I feel almost festive!

*****

Closing the pages, Leah could imagine Linnea's inner thoughts, the things she might not include for others to read:

God bless me, here are my real feelings, unwritten in my diary:

(Dressed in his freshly pressed white shirt, my Thaddeus appears to me the most handsome young man in the room filled with soldiers. I feel like a newlywed—that seems so long ago—when he takes my hand in his, and we waltz to the accompaniment of Colonel Sawyer's accordion. It might be Vienna, as we swirl and leap in light fancy over the saw-dust-strewn floor of the Fort. My Thaddeus is as elegant and desirable to me as he was when I first spied him across the room at Cousin Alice's wedding! How can he be more beautiful as time passes? Is it that I see his strength, understand his depths even more fully as we are so challenged on our voyage together? Is it because he seems so truly manly as he performs his tasks with the wagons? I blush to think how the image of his strong arms and muscled shoulders stirs within me un-biblical feelings, and tonight I am blessed with the thought of privacy.

When Thaddeus puts his arm around my waist and escorts me out of the hall and down the narrow corridor to our tiny room, I am aware of a tremendous longing to be possessed by this man. We close the door, and before he can even turn away from the latch, I have my arms around his back, I am feeling the sinews over his ribs and I turn him around most fiercely. I am utterly hungry for this time with him.

He carries me to the military cot we share, and I don't care that it is dressed with primitive linens, I don't care that this is a rough cell in a remote fort somewhere so far away from all I have ever known. I don't care that the blankets sting my skin as Thaddeus responds to my passion with an urgency and force I have never before felt from him.

I just want to be with him, my man. I forget that we really still have no privacy as I call out in the night. My love. Cherish.)

Chapter Nine

June 26, 1998

L eah tied on the fly and arced the line out over the river. She liked it being so early, liked the feel of the cast, and liked being the only person in this quiet spot. She breathed deeply, deciding her aim had been poor, brought the line in and cast again, this time with the tip of the rod following the correct angle between 10:00 and 1:00, with a softer and better-timed flick of her wrist. She knew of few things that calmed her as much as fishing. She had to admit that the art of fly fishing and catch and release still escaped her, as she had mostly practiced plain old bait fishing with her father and then her brother on boats in the ocean or reservoirs and dams in California until later, when her father had given her a lesson in a different way of fishing, an important memory.

She still recalled the earlier thrill of catching blue gill, perch, or bass and then cooking them for dinner around a campfire. Her years of fishing and camping under her father's and Davey's tutelage had made her expert in the use of a rod and reel. She had even overcome her early reluctance to hook live bait, becoming less squeamish when a tiny cricket put up its arms in protest as she found the spot to insert the hook. She'd gotten positively masculine in her love for the hours spent sitting in a small boat in the middle of a lake or climbing down steep riverbanks in search of a rich school of fish.

This unfeminine love for the challenge of fishing had stood her in good stead when she had sons. She had been the parent who first took her boys to the streams of the Sierras and trained them to look at the way the water flowed to find places fish liked. She was the one who showed them how to yank up at exactly the right time to set the hook in the lip of a large-mouth bass. She was the parent who taught them the etiquette of fishing, of respecting the quiet of other fishermen, of reading the regs carefully and knowing when to release and return fish.

Here she was, on a high-altitude, cold-water stream in Idaho, alone, trying to remember the recent fly-fishing lessons she had treated herself to when she decided to come to the cabin and resume her father's teaching. She practiced her casting rhythm several times, testing the banks and the eddies of the stream. About 7:30 a.m., she brought in her line, set down the rod, and opened her thermos. Hot, strong coffee was one of the absolute pleasures in the world; she reminded herself to be grateful that this particular indulgence hadn't been taken away from her. As it was, she ate virtually no fat, watched her intake of sugar carefully, rarely had any alcohol, and consumed only foods that promoted energy. But she still relished her morning coffee. As the cup warmed her hands in the fingerless gloves, she allowed herself to close her eyes for a minute and just appreciate her time, this very moment, of feeling good. How remarkable!

A male voice disturbed her quiet.

"Mrs. Brown?"

She started. She turned toward the voice, shielded her eyes from the bright early morning sun, and peered up at the dark figure silhouetted against the light.

"Yes?" Her voiced revealed her discomfort.

"It's Adam Caldwell. Sorry if I scared you."

Now she could associate those long legs with the ones she'd stumbled over just a couple of days ago.

"Oh. Hi. I just didn't expect anyone out here at this hour. What are you doing here?"

"Fishing. Like you. I guess you found one of my favorite spots."

Leah noted his gear, minimal and well worn. He had on waders and appeared to have been fishing for a while.

She smiled at him. "Sorry. Well, it was by accident, believe me! I won't tell anyone else about it! Would you like some coffee?"

"No, thanks. But I'll just sit while you have yours."

With that, Adam Caldwell approached the group of rocks holding Leah and sat a few feet away. Leah looked into his face, now that he was no longer backlit by the rising sun.

"Leah. My first name's Leah," she said, offering him a handshake. "I didn't mean to be rude the other day. I was just flustered because of feeling so clumsy."

"That's OK. I got the Mrs. part loud and clear, though. Tell me, what's your husband's name?" Adam smiled, his tone offering no sarcasm.

"Ned. We've been married for sixteen years now." She wondered why she offered the extra information.

Adam looked out at the creek, noticing the currents and the shades of dark where trout might be. They both sat for a few moments until Leah couldn't stand the silence any more.

"Ned runs a small communications company in San Francisco, and I'm its public relations director. I'm just up here for a few weeks, kind of a break."

She watched his reaction, noticing his strong jaw line. Ned had one, too. Funny what things some women found attractive in men. She liked broad shoulders, height, an ease of carriage, the pronounced jaw and big smile. Her friend Till loved hairy chests. She kept her admiration for Adam's chin to herself, averting her eyes when he finally spoke.

"Do you have kids?" Adam asked, and Leah told him all about Tim and Jeff, their summer camp, and how she missed them. They fell into the easy exchange of new acquaintances in new places. She poured another cup of coffee and the minutes passed. The sun rose higher, and as it warmed her, she found it necessary to remove her outer jacket. She felt the press of her breasts against the cotton of her plaid shirt.

She discovered things about Adam. He spent most of his time traveling the Northwest. A writer of nonfiction pieces, mainly about the changing character of the region, he had published a collection of essays, which had received good circulation, and often wrote pieces for major papers in the northwest.

In addition, he had managed to have three of his essays featured in *The New Yorker*; the last one appearing two years ago about the history of the Nez Perce tribe. That piece had required extensive research in and around this region. Adam had traced the boundaries of the reservation, the history of the Native Americans who had remained after the 1877 war, and then followed the lives of those who had left with Chief Joseph.

In his travels, he had sought always to find a retreat, a second home somewhere in the mountains, and had settled on the wild places still untouched along the Payette or Salmon Rivers.

"I can write anywhere, but I enjoy the prospect of spending more time near the wilderness, not having always to camp or find a motel or impose on friends as I explore the mountains. So I'm hoping I can find a small place near here somewhere."

Leah pushed up the sleeve of her flannel shirt and noted the time. They'd been talking for a good half hour now, the dregs of her coffee were cold, and she needed to stretch. As she rose, Adam did also.

"Well," he said, gathering up the gear he'd placed against a small pine tree, "I guess that's enough for today. I'll leave you to your fishing."

Leah sat on the flat rock for a few moments, watching his lanky form retreat along the banks of the river, noting odd, residual feelings visiting her. She reviewed the encounter with Adam, wondering now if her lipstick had been smudged or if her sunblock had been left in smears on her cheeks, aware of her grimy nails. She was unusually self-conscious, on edge, slightly excited, uncomfortable, and even melancholic. After a few moments, she put away her thermos and cup and headed the opposite way up river.

As she resumed her rhythmical series of casts, she entered that safe space between soothing activity and contemplation that fishing usually brought her. She was at peace.

Chapter Ten

"**N**ed? Hi. I'm sorry to call you at work, but I couldn't stand to let more time pass after our conversation."

"That's OK. I'm just clearing off the desk, getting ready to go home." Ned turned his antique swivel chair around so he could put the files on the desk, cradling the office phone between his ear and his right shoulder. Leah would be irritated if he used the speakerphone. "What's up?"

"Nothing, really, except that I'm sorry if I was so snappy. I didn't even get to ask you how the boys were or about the business or anything."

Ned paused long enough to loosen his tie. "So? Are you feeling a little more positive today?"

Leah stifled a small hint of irritation at the tone of his voice. "Yes. Well, that is, I wanted to apologize. I know we've both been under a lot of tension lately." Leah waited for a response, and then continued, "Anyway, I *am* enjoying my solitude." She envisioned a flash of a backlit figure by the river. Not all of her time here was alone, to tell the truth.

"Good" came the grudging response. "You know I still think you should be here with me, but I've given up begging. You only have four and a half weeks left anyway. So what's up?"

"Tell me about the boys and your meeting with Fromley—everything."

Leah leaned back in the sofa, her feet tucked up under her, and listened to Ned's litany. The boys were adjusting beautifully: Tim was enjoying his work with the horses, and Jeff had made a new best friend. As his voice recounted that news and the disappointing decision on Fromley's part tabling acquisition, Leah let herself sit still under the torrent of words from the voice she had heard for so many years.

When Ned finished, he simply said, "So that's about it. Anything new with you?"

"No," she replied, knowing with quick comprehension that some things were new. For some reason she didn't want to share with him her beautiful day, the triumph of catching her first trout with a fly, the reverence she had felt when releasing him to the river, and certainly not the conversation she'd had with Adam. No, all of that could wait. She wanted to enjoy the feeling of healing and reconciliation this phone call meant.

"No," she repeated.

"Well, then, I guess I'll just wait until I hear from you in a few days." Ned swiveled around again, picking up his briefcase. He wanted to hurry away somehow, get on the road, and not listen to his wife another minute. He couldn't understand it, but sensed that something was slipping away, out of his control. So he merely said, "Oh...and, honey. Please read up on the info Dr. Cantrell gave you. We need to talk about your options. I'd like to get started on this end as soon as you make a decision."

"All right," said Leah, wondering why he was pressing her. Why was he back to bugging her about this? Perhaps Mr. Fixit wanted an instant decision. Whatever the reason, in the name of peace, she deferred to his strength, saying merely,

"Thanks for your concern. I'm working on it. Give my love to the boys, OK? And drive carefully. Be safe. Love you."

"Love you too, Leah. Be careful and safe." Ned hung up.

There it was. She was OK. Leah put the phone down and closed her eyes for a minute.

July 2, 1863

Just when I thought we were finally going to get through this dreary part of our trip with some ease, we find ourselves stuck with two wagons losing wheels. The men are, of course, busily trying to determine the damage and making repairs as swiftly as possible. Amanda is asleep at this moment, and I am sitting near the ruined wheel of the wagon. Sometimes, I have to reflect on how much we human beings are held captive by the whims of nature.

My eyes are riveted on the broken wheel by my side. I realize that if the center is not strong, the wheel does not hold. Both the large nut and bolt that securely fix the center are made of a rusted metal that looks everlasting. I imagine them as crafted in a foundry somewhere near my New England home. Their striations and edges are hand-hewn and bear the maker's uneven lined imprint. Their edges seem fused, an amalgamation of surfaces that looks almost seamless.

But I can picture this nut and bolt loosening over the last few weeks, the weight pulling slowly, slowly, and creaking, subtle separation. I can almost see the gradual slipping of metal away from metal, unnoticed by the driver. The cargo's weight stresses the connection. As I write this, I reflect as well on how too much weight always stresses the connections we have as loving human beings. I have noticed husbands being unusually nasty in addressing their wives, who, I can aver, are almost saintly in their endurance. I know that sometime many months or years from now, those same husbands may sit by the comfort of a home-cooked meal at a table set by a warm fire and thank God for their helpmeets, but sometimes, I worry about the couples I am with. Sometimes, I must admit, even my dearest Thaddeus is snappish. I might be tending Amanda and he will want something instantly. When I cannot provide it, he will mutter something unkind, like "Women!" He is used to having me all to himself, and I know that deep down he understands that I didn't ask for this added responsibility, but I honestly don't know how anyone, even a man, can look at this dear girl's eyes and not want to do anything in the world to protect her.

My eyes gaze again at the wheel's center and imagine it slowly slipping, now a fraction of an inch, day by day, until one hard rock hits at a certain angle, and finally the nut and bolt are free of each other. Because of this gradual slipping, we will be stalled for many hours.

Chapter Eleven

July 15

Leah sat outside in the cool evening wrapped in a comforter, her knees tucked up under her. She smelled the delicate scent of anise from the wild-flower patch nearby, reminding her of the Swedish limpa bread her mother had baked for Sunday dinners. The recipe had been handed down for generations; Leah liked the idea that Linnea had baked it here in this part of the world as her mother had in Boston, as her grandmother in Malmo, Sweden, had also baked it. She would bake a loaf for the boys' return from camp.

The stars massed overhead; never had she seen such a show of sparkle in the sky. The summer she got sick might have been as bright, although in those days she seldom had time to sit quietly under the cover of the sky. Then her evenings were filled with easy meals, baths, fastening the seats of cowboy-patterned jammies, reading *Goodnight Moon*, and then waiting until the last sigh and final kiss on her sons' hot cheeks before slipping into some kind of space for herself.

That night, she had been preoccupied with preparations for the opera. A client had given her and Ned eighth row center seats to *La Boheme*, and she had prepared carefully for this rare time out together, its hint of romance and closeness in the dark night of the concert hall especially alluring. She was dressed and almost finished with instructions for the babysitter when she decided to put one more piece of trash in the compactor. Ned was urging her to hurry up, but her compulsive neatness won over reason.

She opened the compactor and, even though seeing it was full, jammed the small plastic piece in with the heel of her hand, and as it stuck in the drawer runner, she felt her right wrist thrust backward on the appliance's sharp metal edges. Blood immediately gushed from the wound, and she wrapped it in a nearby paper towel while Ned got bandages from the bathroom. Because she didn't want to miss the opera, she tried to ignore it, but began to feel frightened when she couldn't seem to stop the gush of blood.

As Ned tried to work a tourniquet and calm the babysitter and the boys, she felt faint, faint enough to say, "Ned. Call 911. Quick!"

The rest of the evening was a blur—Ned's good tourniquet, a neighbor showing up to help, the arrival of the ambulance, leaving her crying children, the blood transfusion, going in and out of consciousness, and the emergency surgery to repair a severed artery. She had been lucky they lived so close to the paramedics' station. Later, she was told that she could have bled out in just a few minutes.

Now, looking back on that experience, Leah reflected on the small turns in life that later prove to have been major shifts in direction. For that hospital stay was most likely the source of her body being invaded by hepatitis C. Little was known about the disease at the time of her transfusion.

Indeed, she had lived blithely for almost seven years after that relatively minor surgery unaware that her blood harbored a potentially dangerous villain, that damage to her liver was occurring even as she left Jeff in his first kindergarten class, watched Tim play center field in Little League, and saw him grow four inches in one semester of the sixth grade. In fact, it wasn't until the "moving up" ceremonies noting the transition of his class to junior high that she first began to feel sick.

As she sat that day under that unshaded June sun, envisioning the straw hat still on the entry table where she had placed it so she wouldn't forget, she felt a clench in her stomach, a piercing sense of nausea, and overall body aches. She was afraid that she would have to stumble out through the bright blue wooden lawn chairs in her long row on the elementary school playground grass, but the intense feeling passed. Only when she rose to honor the graduates with applause did she again feel the fist in her stomach. This time, it made her dizzy.

Ascribing her illness to the flu, Leah successfully ignored this first sign of disease. In August of that year, when she and the family were at Stinson Beach, she noticed that her hands and feet looked yellowish. However, she put aside her qualms until the weekend when, in the bright sun off the ocean streaming into the bathroom window of the small rental house, she saw that her eyes were also tinged with a sickly yellow pallor. During the remainder of their stay at the beach, Leah catalogued the signs of what she now recognized as an illness. She *had* lost her appetite lately, along with a few pounds. She *had* been lethargic, even a little bit spacey. She *had* been off in many ways.

The following week, she saw her family doctor. He referred her to John Cantrell, a specialist in liver disease. Then she underwent a series of tests, including a liver screening, ultrasound scan, and a liver biopsy, which she now thought of as one of the most unpleasant procedures she had ever experienced. Although she realized her good fortune at living near San Francisco General, where she knew her problems would be diagnosed correctly, she still shuddered at the memory of the liver biopsy.

She tried to be accurate when recalling her discomfort to Ned.

"Oh, god. It was awful! They put me on my back and gave me a local anesthetic, and then Dr. Cantrell took a long thin needle and inserted it just below my ribs. You know, where I've been so bloated.

"I had to hold my breath while they put the needle into my liver and took some of the tissue for the lab. I was supposed to remain still through this part of the procedure because they didn't want to lacerate the liver." She paused, remembering the strain of her efforts.

Ned was stroking her forehead as she told him about the procedure. They were lying together on the fat couch in their ninety-year old hillside home in Sausalito. It took up most of the floor of the small living room and was placed so they could enjoy the view of the bay. Sometimes, Leah felt like she and Ned were on a boat when they cuddled this way, the blue water seen at this angle looked the same way the water did from the deck of their sloop. He leaned down and kissed her just above her eyelid, what they termed a butterfly kiss.

His reply was simple. "Oh, honey! You must have been so uncomfortable."

"I was really concentrating on being absolutely quiet. I felt a sharp stab but did manage to keep myself still. After they took out the needle, they asked me to lie on my right side. Oddly, during the six hours I stayed at the clinic, I experienced a really bad pain in my right shoulder. Weird. It hurt so much so that Dr. Cantrell eventually gave me some pain-killers. Doesn't that seem strange?"

"Not really, honey," Ned said. "When I came to pick you up, I asked them about your discomfort. They told me that happens to many patients. Anyway, it's over now and the best thing is that we'll know what we're dealing with."

Of course, it wasn't over, none of it. Later that afternoon, when Dr. Cantrell told her she had hepatitis C, it was merely the beginning.

Chapter Twelve

July 20, 1998

Dear Tim and Jeff,

Thank you for the postcards. Daddy sent them on to me to read, and I must say I am proud of you both. I bet you've both grown so much! When you are with someone every day it's hard to notice, but being away from you for the summer will probably make it really obvious to me. I can imagine both of you getting big muscles and being very tan after all of your swimming!

By now, I bet you have received the pictures I sent you of the cabin. You would really enjoy this place, and I think we should plan a trip up here next summer (unless someone buys it—you know, Grandma has put it on the market.)

The best news! I did catch a trout the other day. It was a beautiful rainbow, about ten inches long and quite fat. Of course, I released him back to the river, and I swear he gave me a friendly look just before I did. There are also some reservoirs within driving distance, and if you come up next summer, we will get some dinner fish. Maybe we can all learn more together about the art of fly-fishing. As you know, I am not very sentimental about fish, but I am beginning to see why people love this sport so much. I am planning on fishing again tomorrow. I must say this has been really fun.

I hope you are enjoying the cookies Grandma sent.

I am feeling good and rested here away from the office. Daddy says that things are going quite all right without me, so I feel very lucky to have this quiet time alone. Whatever I decide to do next about my illness, remember that you mean so much to me, and I always want to hear your thoughts.

Every time I look up into the clear, bright night, I think of you and remember that time we studied astronomy with the guide at Family Camp in Pinecrest. Do you remember how much we talked about the vastness of the universe? Here, the sky is so clean that I even feel closer to Ursa Major, the North Star, and the Little Dippers. I have named two of the brightest stars Tim and Jeff, and when they sparkle at me, I can see your smiles.

I love you so much! XXXOOO

Mom

*****

Leah popped half of an oatmeal cookie in her mouth and was sealing the envelope when she heard footsteps approaching. She put the letter down and went to the door. When she creaked the thick door open, she noticed first a middle-aged woman with salt-and-pepper curly hair, and then, behind her, Adam Caldwell.

He loomed at least a foot taller than the lady, who said, "Mrs. Brown? I'm sorry to bother you, but we have no phone number for you." She extended her hand. "I'm Betty Andreason from Mountain Realty. I guess I missed you the other day."

"Oh, hi. Of course! I'm forgetting my manners." She opened the door wider. "You're the first visitors I've had."

She felt rattled, for some reason. "I probably seem a bit unsocial, but I just needed some quiet time here. Oh, well."

Here she was again, supplying a plethora of information. "Please come in."

Leah stepped back and allowed Mrs. Andreason and Adam to come into the dark room.

"Can I make you some tea? I don't have any soft drinks."

She imagined she might have crumbs on her chin or a runny nose or something embarrassing. She wished she'd had time to check her reflection in the mirror.

"No thanks," the real estate woman replied. "I understand you've met Mr. Caldwell before. He is looking at several places in this area, and I thought since we were in the neighborhood, we'd stop by."

Leah nodded in Adam's direction, acknowledging their having already met. "Sure. That's fine."

She turned to study Adam, who was politely holding his Stetson in his hand like some Jimmy Stewart cowboy. She noticed him glancing around the living area. The room looked very small to her, as his presence seemed to fill it up.

"Please. Just feel free to wander around. There's not a whole lot more to see."

Leah was glad she was a creature of habit: she'd at least pulled the comforter up over the bed; all her life she had done that as soon as she put her feet on the floor. She could hear her mother saying that as long as you had an unmade bed or dirty dishes in the sink, you could consider yourself a slob. She looked at the kitchen counter. Sure enough, there were dirty cups from the morning still unwashed, silent sentinels guarding the sink and attesting to her slovenliness! *For god's sake!* she told herself. *This is not some Beverly Hills mansion. It's just a simple cabin for roughing it. Stop the California good girl habit!* She inadvertently blushed at the good girl reference. *Why those words?*

Looking at the imposing figure of Adam Caldwell, she knew the reason. When she glanced up at his clear blue eyes, she momentarily wondered what it would feel like to press herself up against that lean frame.

She heard Mrs. Andreason prattling on about the age of the cabin, its history, saw Adam politely nodding his head, and stilled her heart a bit when they left the main room to look at the bedroom. She didn't know what to do with the couple of minutes before they returned and finally sat at the table and busied herself with the envelope once again, as if she had just now thought to seal and stamp it. When they returned, she acted as though suddenly surprised by their presence, although she hadn't spent one second without con-juring up the picture of those long legs, the Levi jacket, and the man with the well-worn hat in hand.

"Well, once again, thank you," she heard Mrs. Andreason say. "We'll be on our way. Do you mind if we just walk around the property for a bit? Kind of show my client where the boundaries are?"

"Of course. Whatever you need. Just let me know." She arose and faced them.

The realtor turned to the door and started to leave but stopped for a moment while Adam spoke.

"Mrs. Brown." he said. "I just want to add my thanks for your tolerance of our unannounced visit. Thank you."

"You're most welcome," Leah said, accompanying them to the door.

Adam followed Mrs. Andreason out the door, and just as it was about to close, Leah swore she heard him whisper when he started to turn the knob. "Fishing tomorrow?"

70

The house suddenly seemed empty for the first time since she had arrived.

*****

July 3, 1863

We are in Idaho Territory, desolate country with nothing but sagebrush and wind around us. It is almost hard now to recall the joy we felt at Fort Laramie. The oxen are tired and thirsty, and we needed to lighten our loads in order to help them survive. Just yesterday, at a bend in the river, I had to leave the dresser of my childhood. It was the place I used to hide my little trinkets and the rocks I would gather from my play in the fields near my home. I almost cannot bear the thought of leaving it behind, but Mr. Price has convinced us that our four oxen are weakening and that we cannot hold on to these selfish reminders of the past. He tells me that I should remember that I am a pioneer, and that my new life will be fresh and full of promise. Still, I allowed myself a few moments to study its lines and etch it in my memory. I looked at it for many minutes after we unloaded it. The clunky but beloved old thing sat in the increasing distance, getting smaller and smaller in my vision. I could make out its contours for a long time until they finally merged with the waves of heat and light and the dimming lines of vegetation. At each of the pulls of our four charges, Bessie, Bobby, Bountiful, and Ben, I hoped those beasts stepped a bit quicker and lighter as we put the distance between us and my beloved childhood.

Last week along the Sweetwater, there was a section where we saw graves every eighty to one hundred yards. One of them had been dug up, apparently by wolves, and we could see part of a skull sticking up in the disturbed dirt. When we stopped for dinner that night, one of the other men in the train told of seeing a wolf with a comb and what must have been human hair in its mouth. I hope my dear friend Helen, alone out there in the plains, sleeps in an undisturbed grave.

Tonight, as I tuck in Amanda, I will say my nightly prayer for Helen. Perhaps I can rekindle her special spirit and be more accepting in my journey with her baby. We must keep our eyes on the future. I can hold the center if I pray for the faith to endure each piece of time that God gives me. After all, I have survived another day!

*****

Leah put down the diary and got out of bed to take her medicine and brush her teeth. It was only 9:00 at night, but she felt more weary than usual. Perhaps she had lost her hold on the center of things. As she turned off the lamp before hunkering under the comforter, she focused on her needed rest for her day of fishing tomorrow.

Chapter Thirteen

July 21

Leah's back ached, and she reluctantly put her fishing gear away as she saw that the sun was getting low in the sky. She had planned to fish earlier in the day but instead spent some time with the literature Dr. Cantrell had given her. She actually preferred fishing later, hoping that twilight would yield more opportunities to catch trout. She had certainly tried early morning enough and even experimented with different flies she'd acquired from the tackle box that had belonged to her father.

Now as she placed the Adams Mayfly back into the section for trout flies, briefly stroking the smooth fibers, she could almost hear her father speak. *Daddy.*

*****

Daddy is unlocking the key to a shabby motel, its paint peeling off in the high desert August sun of Bishop. Davey was left at home, so she had him all to herself. Their vacation began a few moments earlier when she stepped off the bus from San Francisco to be caught high against his strong chest. She felt his stubbly chin as he hugged her tight and kissed her on her forehead. *Daddy.*

Even the small room is magical because he is here. At the diner next door with the flashing neon sign "Eat Here!" the grilled cheese sandwiches taste better than anything prepared at home.

"Cookie?" Daddy says, "Tomorrow we're going hiking, and then I have a special surprise for you."

They spend the first few days together exploring the foothills of the Sierra Mountain range, even walking so high that they encounter small patches of snow under the overhanging branches of huge sequoias.

One day, they rent a small boat and row out on Lake Crowley, an oasis in the dry surroundings, and catch enough perch so that Daddy is able to cook them for dinner over the small Coleman stove he carries in his truck.

"Sweetie, I think you are ready to do some fly fishing with me. I've been waiting until you were just a little older because I want you to like it. How about it?"

"Sure, Daddy." His red and black flannel shirt is soft as she leans against his arm. "Tomorrow?"

She remembers that next day as if it were today: after getting coffee for Daddy's thermos and donuts for the road, they drive up to Mammoth Lakes and then up winding roads as far as the truck can go. Daddy has a wooden tackle box with him and two different fishing rods without the kind of reels they have used before.

They hike way up high, to about nine thousand feet above sea level, unlike the flat palaces where she and Mommy live. The air is thin and she is tired, but her father finally stops just when she is about to give up.

When Daddy opens the tackle box, she covets the bright flies and their many varieties of colors and shapes. With her father's arms holding hers, she learns to cast the line and retrieve it as it catches in branches along the banks of high mountain streams.

Her first lesson in catching and releasing comes about 4:30, just as the sun is slipping against the back of the mountains, the sunset bronzing the highest peaks.

She feels the tug on the fine line.

"Daddy. Come quick! I've got something!"

He father puts down his gear and helps her reel in the lively fish, and as she watches him bring it in, she wants to keep it, to study the iridescent scales, and examine the silver miracle. She has seen dead trout in markets before. But they never looked as shimmery and magical as this. Death robs them of their brightness. But her father unhooks the fish and lets it swim back into the clear waters, its tail shimmying with a sure speed.

Then after many days that pass as swiftly as the trout returning to the stream, days that, in memory, seem illusory and evanescent, her summer time with her father is over. Too soon, she boards the Greyhound for San Rafael. Before she follows her suitcase up the steep steps of the bus, her father gives her a final hug and presents her with the tackle box.

"Here," he says. "I want you to keep this until we can be together again. You are the custodian of this box."

As the bus pulls away, Leah looks out the window at her father's figure getting smaller and smaller. *Daddy*.

*****

Well, no Daddy now. She pulled the metal clasp over the knob, picked up the tackle box and, zipping up her forest green windbreaker, turned away from the river, and headed toward the cabin. Through the undergrowth, she sensed movement and drew back. As she ducked under an overhanging cottonwood branch, Adam pushed through the foliage. She hadn't heard him, though she had, she realized, been listening for him all day.

"Oh. Hi! I'm glad it's you," she said, astonished at how glad she was.

"Sorry," he said, noting her alarm. He looked at her gear packed for day's end. "Guess I missed fishing with you."

Leah didn't respond, just looked down at brush lining the river's edge. His waders were worn, recalling her father's. How could she bear the memories?

*****

In her frilly yellow-and white bedroom at home the tackle box had held an honored place. Leah kept it on the pull-down desk next to her diary and Storybook Doll suitcase. Every once in a while, she would take it to her bed and flatten a square on her quilt for it. She would first rub the smooth edges where the sides of the box had been cunningly joined by a grid of wood pieces fitting together like teeth. Her father's smell always returned to her when she did that. Then she would take out the dozens of flies, arranging them according to color or size, imagining tying them with the knots her father used, awaiting the next time she could board the big Greyhound Bus and head south across Donner Pass to see her father.

Only as a grown-up did Leah understand why her father had entrusted her with his tackle box. It had never occurred to her at the age of eight that there was a reason he wouldn't be using it himself. Even when her mother received the phone call a few weeks later from Grandma, and Leah heard her shrieks, she still didn't understand.

Later, at the funeral services, she overheard some lady talking about how her father had died of carbon monoxide poisoning in his old Studebaker, his body found among the cases of pens and pencils and small advertising giveaways he'd started to sell out of his car. She still didn't connect the gift of the tackle box with her father's plans to die. It would take years before she understood the truth. Then, one day, when she was packing for college, she found the dusty wooden box, by now up on a closet shelf, and she could swear that the smell of his Old Spice aftershave still lingered amidst the more acrid odors associated with fishing gear. She took it with her to college, and next to her chemistry and French textbooks, the tackle box was a legacy, a daily reminder of her father. Instead of being sad when she saw it each time she entered her dorm room, Leah used it as a talisman. It would remind her to cherish life always and never ever leave her children bereft.

Now she saw it again as the gift it was.

Several years after her father's suicide, a friend of hers wrote a poem when *her* father died, and Leah had kept a copy of that poem in the tackle box. During her time as a young mother, she had memorized it, wishing that her father had chosen to live long enough to know the love of his grandchildren. Later, when she was so ill, she actually memorized the poem, embedding in her memory the love of another daughter in a different place and time. She could see it now, more relevant than ever:

Daddy's Lap

Daddy has a lap:
full, comforting, and safe.
I lean my head against his chest,
ringlets felt through Oxford cloth,
a woven textile of love
for me to rest upon.

Brylcreem and Old Spice, cheap sherry and Bubble Up:
Daddy in the garden on hot Burbank nights,
his cigarette a firefly
between the orange eyes of birds of paradise,
scents of camellias and Mother's roses.
The sweetness overwhelmed.

Tickle of mustache on my forehead,
flesh that jiggled with laughter
at ZaSu Pitts and Abbott and Costello, "Mississippi Mud"
played on our upright,
Daddy's eyes rolling.
I snuggle next to him on the mahogany bench.

Long gone from earth my father's love,
the altar of his arms,
His days in radio when I'd lean into his blue serge suit
and speak into the mike.
His dreams for me blended into early pride:
Always an audience, a birthright fan club,
approval, tenderness, and adulation.

I've searched for Daddy's lap in men at distance,
men who told me of my charms,

men who held me loosely in their arms.
Never the same sense of place,
of fitting in the large and generous space
of Daddy's lap.

Adam reached out to offer his arm.

"Maybe you'll let me walk you home. It is getting dark."

In answer, Leah smiled. Adam took her elbow as they walked up the riverbank toward the path home.

Far in the distance, Leah heard the howl of some creature. She looked up at Adam.

Finally, she said, "I hadn't realized how fast the darkness hits. What's your favorite animal?" She found herself asking him, still aware of the sounds of creatures in the incipient night.

"I don't know," he replied, looking sideways at her and smiling. "That's a bit like asking me to select my favorite book. Almost impossible. Why'd you ask?"

"Oh, I guess just because I was listening to that wolf or whatever. You know the way people choose dogs that resemble themselves? I think it says something about you." She looked back up at him, shy. "Oh, hell. Truth? I was just filling the quiet." She stepped slightly closer to him.

"Wait. Look over there." Adam pointed across a meadow to a thicket of trees on the other side. Two deer stood grazing at the edge of the brush. They looked up, nostrils flaring.

"I never tire of seeing even animals as familiar as deer," he said, after they had stood quietly for a few minutes.

"They are beautiful," Leah responded.

"OK," Adam said, now taking his arm from her elbow and putting it around her shoulder, "my favorite animal is the antelope. I can't think of anything more spectacular than a herd of antelope conquering one of the rolling hills of the West. Once in Sun Valley I was surprised to see about twenty of them loping along the top of the ski mountain. It seemed funny, how totally unaware they were of being an anomaly in the land of Lycra, hard bodies and high-tech gear. So what's yours?"

"Mine? No contest. I adore elephants. They're such wonderful, awkward, sweet creatures. I probably love them because they're so fiercely loyal and family oriented. I've felt close to them ever since I saw a show about their behavior when one of their herd died, circling in grief around the fallen female."

Leah threw back her head a bit, looking for Adam's eyes in the darkening sky.

She was half-amazed and half-expectant when he leaned down to meet her face and kissed her. Leah felt the soft pressure of the unfamiliar lips, felt the surprising softness of his kiss, then melted into a deeper kiss. For just a moment, she fell into the cliché of first kisses: she forgot where she was.

The last time she felt this had been too long ago, but it was with her husband. She pulled away, not wanting to.

"I'm sorry, Adam, but I don't think I can do this. I *am* married."

"I know. I'm sorry." He wiped his mouth with the back of his jacket, turned away, and again led her by her elbow along the path.

They didn't speak again until they reached Leah's door.

"Thanks for the walk home. I should probably ask you in for coffee…"

"No, you shouldn't," he interrupted. "I understand."

And leaning down, he kissed her softly on the forehead and turned away down the long driveway.

Leah went inside and, without even turning on her lights, walked directly to her bedroom, where she sat on the edge of the bed and cried.

That night, she dreamed of the African veldt, of the Serengeti, of gazelles and antelope and emus and swift creatures leaping across marshy grass in bursts of life. The blurred shapes beckoned in their speed, promising an escape from the confines of the human form, of responsibility, of ties to the things of this world.

Chapter Fourteen

Leah was at last allowing herself to enjoy her husband's touch. Ned's fingers pressed on the soft spot between her toes and then moved over to the pressure points under her arches. She closed her eyes, feeling his strong, thick fingers, letting the tingles spread across her scalp, the relaxation seep in, the mean thoughts ebb away from her analytical mind. She had almost sent him home. The idea that his unannounced visit was a violation kept interfering with the conversation they had been having since Ned arrived just before dinner.

She had been reading the diary when she heard a car come down the long dirt driveway. She didn't stir because she assumed someone had made a wrong turn, but the engine stopped and a door opened. Her first thought was Adam. She arose from the sofa, put the heavy journal on the coffee table, and went to the door, just as Ned knocked.

"Ned! What are you doing here?" she had exclaimed. His arms were loaded with grocery bags. She let him in.

He looked at her with an askew grin as he placed the bags on the counter.

"I know, I know, you asked me not to phone, but you didn't say anything about just showing up."

"I don't know what to say." Leah found herself almost unable to give him a hug or kiss. She went to him, let him hold her fiercely and then kiss her even as her mind pondered signals of betrayal. This was so like Ned. Here he was, big and warm and vibrant and strong. If she complained about his presence, she would seem ungrateful, would just hurt his feelings. And wordsmith that he was, he would convince her that indeed they had never talked about his not *coming* here. Besides, he must have driven forever.

So instead of carping about his presence, Leah simply said, "How long have you been driving? You must be tired."

"Not long." He tossed his head at an angle to indicate the SUV parked out of her eyesight. "Not bad, really." He looked into her eyes, squeezing her harder. "I stopped and got some food and a bottle of good wine. You'll have half a glass, won't you? Let's celebrate my being here, OK?"

Her objections to his spontaneous trip seemed petty and mean-spirited. After all, he was her husband, would support her always, and had done this out of love and good motives.

While they talked about the boys and the minutiae of domestic living, they fell into the familiar banter, the sharing of all the little things. He found the potato peeler and took over his usual chore.

And now, with the last remnants of merlot in the glasses reflecting the glow of the fireplace behind, blazing with unusual summer fire, she tried to accept everything else that had followed, to put it aside and savor the moment.

"So," Ned had said, raising his glass of wine in a toast, "here's to our merger with Fromley Associates. As soon as you get back, we'll seal the deal."

"Why didn't you consult me?" she said, even though she had been the one to insist on the distance they had developed these past few weeks.

Ned studied her.

"It's an offer I don't think we can afford to pass up. Fromley's been wanting to open a West Coast office for a long time, and when I really thought about it, I decided that I'm not ready to let go. We still need the medical benefits, for example."

Ned sipped the dregs of his first glass of wine and broke the loaf of San Francisco sourdough into a fist-sized piece, handing it to Leah.

"Anyway, I think I can stick with the operations for a couple of more years and then make an exit."

Leah and Ned had spent the rest of dinner poring over the details of Fromley's offer, and Leah found herself getting caught up in the excitement of the project.

Now here, on the couch with her legs over Ned's thighs, she looked at her husband's closed eyes as he pressed his fingers into her high arches. He actually enjoyed rubbing her feet. How lucky she was even for this small quality of his. When she was pregnant, they would spend every evening on their couch just as they were doing now, Ned kneading her tired feet, while they pondered their future, the names of their children, the dreams they had for their family. And through all the hideous time on Interferon, Ned had continued this. She supposed it wasn't that big a favor in the context of all of the things Ned had done and would continue doing for her, but right now, with the firelight dancing off his curly hair, his thick-lashed eyes masking whatever thoughts he might be entertaining, his hands giving her pleasure, she was content. It was a big little thing.

Only when he began to move his hands up her calves did she switch back to an awareness of her previous irritation. Why couldn't this just be a massage by itself?

Leah reflected on the times she had loved this happening—that a soothing massage became an erotic one, that Ned could get her completely relaxed and ready for the further exploration of his fingers and caresses. Now, though, she was annoyed. She didn't feel like making love; that was it.

The lovemaking that she and Ned had once known had all but disappeared for a combination of reasons. There was the inevitable advance of years with an attendant routine and a sense of familiarity and now a lack of spontaneity; they kidded each other with the phrase "always on Sundays," but it was true. They had made love during her treatments on the one day a week she felt strong enough; then, after she stopped having shots, they continued the habit, partially because she still had symptoms. Then there was the necessity of condoms since her diagnosis.

Most of all, though, her interest in sex had somehow vanished, and she resented Ned's refusing to remember this, putting her in the spot of having to reject him. Like an unwanted pinch, she recalled the erotic touch of Adam's kiss but squelched any thoughts of the slip she had made. Why couldn't she just respond to her husband? Why couldn't she turn off her mind and take pleasure in their history together, in the future she knew would be with this man? She felt a stiffening inside her chest. A term she had once heard, "hardness of heart," popped into her mind. Wasn't it Nathaniel Hawthorne who felt that was the worst sin? And here she was, letting the edges of her heart atrophy into brittle barriers against the man who had been so good to her.

She feigned sleep, feeling sneaky and lousy and adrift all at the same time, but Ned didn't get the hint. Now she peeked through her almost-shut lids and saw that he was looking at her body, that as he kneaded her thighs beneath the denim skirt she had been wearing, he was pulling it up and focusing on the faint tan line just below the edge of her panties.

"Ned," she finally said. "Ned."

But he wasn't listening. Now he was moving forward to hold her in his arms. As he leaned down to kiss her, she relented. But she felt nothing. *Damn it,* she thought. *What is the matter with me?*

"Ned. Ned! Stop."

Ned pulled back, the shock of her words evident on his face. He pushed her further into the couch, stood up, smoothed her skirt around her legs, and turned away from her.

"Ned. I'm sorry." She was unable to say anything more.

Ned went to his small duffel and unzipped it, still avoiding her eyes.

She tried again. "Ned. I'm sorry. I just…well, you know. It's not you. I don't know what's the matter. Please. Let's take a walk or something."

He still didn't look at her.

"Ned. Please. Look at me. Please."

He turned now, his eyes veiled and dark. "What do you want from me? Did I come here to be insulted? We haven't seen each other for over six weeks. I've certainly missed *you.* What is the matter with you?"

Leah arose from the couch and went over to him. She put her arms around him, feeling the heat of his body against her breasts.

"I don't know, darling. Please forgive me. Let's just take a walk and then go to bed. Maybe it's the medicine. We've been through this before. It's not you. Please."

"You know, Leah, I don't feel like walking. I'm tired. I'm going to go take a shower and go to sleep. I'll get out of your hair—and your bed—early in the morning."

As Ned took his duffel into the bedroom, Leah went over to the sink, rinsed the dishes, and decided to overcome her stupid resentments.

*****

By the time she joined him in bed, Ned was turned on his side, facing the wall. She slipped under the covers and held him from behind, caressing his furry chest and admiring his warmth and male skin. She rubbed his chest for several minutes, then in the dark of the still Idaho night, let her hands touch the rest of his body. When he finally turned to her, she was no longer irritated; she could be consumed by gratitude for his presence and be ready for his responses. She could be good to him. She closed her eyes tight and practiced a relaxation technique, noting each of her five senses, coming alive to touch and smell and taste. She let herself enjoy the sound of his heavy breathing.

"Darling, darling Ned," she whispered.

When she looked up at the ceiling during his most passionate kisses, she was distracted by an image of a tall figure wearing waders. Again, she removed any thought of Adam from her mind and concentrated on trying to feel fulfilled. After Ned turned over, she didn't even let the knowledge that she was faking a passion she didn't feel disturb her thoughts. Part of her wanted to speak again with Ned about her fears, but unsolicited honesty was not appropriate at this moment. She hoped the night could heal some of the tension between them, make her feel less of a traitor. Nor did she let the knowledge that he hadn't once asked about her health diminish the solace of this moment. She was surprised at how deeply she slept next to her husband, her Ned.

*****

She closed the heavy old door and moved to the window, watching the back of the car as Ned drove away. She felt a wave of nausea, that familiar feeling from her illness but also the same churnings she had always felt when her conscience was disturbed. Something queasy, something unsettling, something ignoble about her behavior since Ned's arrival stirred inside her.

When she was little and told a fib or as a teenager engaged in malicious gossip, she had experienced the same sensation. It was her "Jiminy Cricket syndrome," as her mother said the time Leah confessed that she and her closest girlfriends had snubbed a homely girl who lived around the corner. She knew when she got that feeling that she had done something less than honorable; as an adult, she called it an emotional hangover.

Whether from a damaged liver or from the damage she'd done to her marriage, the rolling eddies of pain inside her were increasing. She went to the kitchen sink, filled with the remnants of their breakfast, put some water in the teapot, and waited for it to boil.

She thought about her great-grandmother's sense of honor, so obvious on every page. Did she share that quality? How much of Linnea's story was hers? Perhaps her account of a life of challenge could give her some perspective. She opened the diary.

Chapter Fifteen

July 10, 1863

*T*hank God we are safely at Fort Hall! The unremitting dust and wind has finally gotten us all down, I believe. While I am grateful we are here, I also fear that the rest of the voyage will be more difficult because we must say goodbye to ten of our wagons. They've chosen to take a different route and head for California when we approach the Raft River at Pacific Springs. I am weary.

We did have one delightful surprise during our recent travail. We stopped for water at Soda Springs, a place well marked for us by previous prairie schooners. Our predecessors left messages extolling the virtues of this water, and they said that when the liquid was mixed with citrus syrup and sugar, it would create a lemonade so delicious that it redeemed some of the hardships of our voyage. I can testify to that fact. In truth, we were so delighted with the nectar that even my sober Thaddeus admitted a broad smile on his usually dour countenance. And little Amanda laughed and smiled so when she swallowed the fizzy water, that I almost forgot that her mother could not be with us to enjoy the sight.

Actually, it is because of Amanda that I am most sad now. Her unhappy father has determined to split from us and go on to California, and I must admit that I will miss caring for her. I do not know how Josiah will manage without my help, but *perhaps there is some other woman who will step forward to offer a hand. I have even thought of asking him if we should continue to care for Amanda and take her with us until such a time as he would be settled and come to get her, but I fear we could lose touch somehow, that the distance would prove too great. I also think Josiah might be insulted. I know he loves Amanda dearly and will always want to be her father.*

There is another reason I will not press my suit for Amanda. I do think I may be with child. I have not experienced the curse for two months now and am not as interested in food as I was even as short a time ago as Fort Laramie. I do not want to tell Thaddeus yet and will wait until I am sure.

I also hope there may be a doctor at Fort Boise, for by the time we arrive there, if I am with child, I will be in my third or fourth month and thus more secure that I can bear the child for the full term. By that time, we will be two-thirds of the way through our trip and able to plan for our settling.

*****

The day the doctor confirmed her pregnancy, Leah ran down the steps of the office building fronting Market Street with such elation that she must have resembled Rocky leaping on the steps in Philadelphia. She could hardly contain her excitement. For days now, she had harbored her suspicions, occasionally allowing the prospect of motherhood to slip in the back of her mind even as she was making a presentation for a client as powerful as the association of Napa-Sonoma vintners. While extolling the subtleties of the new harvest of Chardonnay, she would experience a totally unexpected clench of joy. It felt like she was having secret and happy sex, the kind you didn't talk about but pondered when a dull office routine would allow a few minutes for the contemplation of delight.

Leah had always wanted to be a mother but in some unexplained way had doubted that she would. Maybe every woman had these misgivings, but she was sufficiently superstitious not to even mention the skipped period to Ned. She felt afraid to tell the news before it was certain.

Now, though, she ran to the bus, ran to the apartment off Green Street, ran up the steps to the nook they had occupied since their wedding in the old Victorian converted clapboard overlooking the Marina. She wanted to rush also to the telephone, to tell Ned, to give him the sensation of instant joy she was feeling, but disciplined herself to cook a dinner of fettuccini from the deli around the corner, cool the Chardonnay she'd received as a sample, change out of her work clothes into a velour lounging outfit, and bring out the lovely Italian porcelain her sister had given them as a wedding present.

When Ned walked in, he knew something was special but waited until dessert to ask, "OK. What's up?"

Leah had practiced a clever little recitation, maybe even a poem for the occasion but just blurted out, "I'm pregnant!"

In all of her years of watching sappy movies and television sitcoms, Leah had seen the more banal male responses to such an announcement. Would Ned lapse into silence, his Adam's apple broadcasting his unease? Would he leap up and shout with joy to the heavens as one Italian actor she had seen did? Would he cover up a horrible feeling of burdensome responsibility by a lukewarm reaction?

Thank God, Ned did none of these. He simply put his hand across the table to cup hers, look deeply into her eyes, and said, "I can't think of anyone I would rather have as the mother of my children. Thank you."

How good he had been!

*****

July 20

 I have forgotten to honor my writing recently, as we have been through the most terrible passage along the Snake River. It is most frustrating to be in our line of wagons and hear water rushing near us only to find it so difficult to obtain! Every time we need more water, we have to stop by the high and precipitous banks of the river and wait for a long time while the most agile among us take perilous routes down the steep embankments and haul up small buckets of water. The gorge is very steep and seems never to become shallower, and we have already seen men fall on the sharp rocks and boulders lining the river. Except for that water, the rest of the landscape seems to consist entirely of barren fields of sagebrush. I admit to being most uncomfortable in many ways.

 In addition, I am even now more convinced that I bear life within me. I feel my dress seams straining against my thickening waist. I still haven't told Thaddeus, as he is so tired from being one of the men who regularly climb up and down the gorge when necessary. He seems to have gotten quieter since Josiah left. He tells me that he is merely concentrating on our destination and all it takes to get us there, but I wish he could find it within him to speak a little more to me than in the short commands he seems to employ more and more. When he finally puts his head down on the pillow at night, he is so tired that he barely turns to me to say God Bless.

*****

Again, Leah superimposes the underlying truth:

(I cannot believe that I am thinking these thoughts, but I am fearful of Thaddeus's visit tonight. When he is tired, instead of simply falling asleep in my arms, he often turns to me with a ferocity that is new between us. The first time he roused me from my sleep after he came late to our bed, I imagined he would spend some time telling me about the efforts he had expended or share some of the stories that pass between the men as they work. Instead, he threw me over and lay on top of me, loving me roughly and quickly. I hardly had time to give him the sweet kisses we usually exchange before he asserted his will on mine. I am unhappy with this turn of events and wonder now if I might have stimulated this more primitive quality in him by my show of desire at Fort Hall. I hope this is temporary and only a sign of his frustrations with the slow passage of our train. Please, dear God, return to me the tender man he was. I must blow out the candle and pretend that I sleep. Perhaps he will not interrupt my sleep.)

****

July 21

I must stop being so querulous. Perhaps it is just because I, too, miss the company of those who left. I miss Amanda's baby kisses, her downy little tuft of hair, and her tiny arms around my neck. I know the path we are on is right, but sometimes I think of my friends who have gone on to the golden shores of California, where it is reputed to be warm and amenable in weather. I know we are facing cold winters and a harsher climate. If this sagebrush is any indication, I shall not find it as much to my liking as I would have hoped.

*****

Leah put the diary aside while she went to the bathroom. She had just experienced another wave of nausea. When it passed, she drank a little water. She decided to lie down for a while and just let her emotions settle. She felt more acutely than ever a kinship with Linnea. Alone, pregnant, and with an ill and uncommunicative husband, Linnea had not had the options she, as a twentieth century woman, had. And yet, feeling the empty spaces on the comforter beneath her, Leah had felt more alone than she had ever been. In truth, she could not communicate with anyone either, certainly not about her irritation with Ned, nor about the irresponsible flirtation she had engaged in with Adam, and really, not even about her choices concerning her illness. She returned to bed and picked up the diary again.

***

Fort Boise
August 1

We are fortunate to have arrived at this oasis, but I am nonetheless very worried. Our almost three hundred miles along the rock-strewn south rim of the Snake River is over. However, four days ago, feeling that he now knew how to master the banks of the river, Thaddeus tripped and severely injured his leg when he landed on a massive boulder. While the men had to move him up, he screamed with such intensity and pain that I became alarmed. His left leg was hideously twisted, and by the time he and his bearers reached the top of the precipice, Thaddeus had fainted. Mr. Price set the leg in a temporary splint, and I have tended to him as best I could during the last few days.

Now that we are at Fort Boise, Thaddeus has been able to see a doctor, Major Barrett. The injury, by mischance, is to the same leg he injured as a child, and the doctor said that it will thus take more time to heal correctly. I'm afraid that the doctor says he must not go on with the wagon train when it departs in two days; this news prompted the most ungracious diatribe from my husband. However, we must abide by the orders of Major Barrett, a fine man who is stationed with the army here and tended Yankee soldiers during the early days of the Civil War. Thus, he knows of what he speaks, and I'm sure that when Thaddeus gets over his initial disappointment, he will understand that he can be of no use on a wagon train or anywhere else until he is whole.

And so, of course, I still have not found the right moment to tell my dear husband that he must care for himself, as he is to be a father next February or March. The good doctor confirmed my sense that it is so.

I do not know what we will do after our friends and travel companions in those remaining wagons bound for Oregon have left. They must continue without us; they cannot wait, as they must get to their destinations while the weather is still warm and they can build shelter and make ready for the winter. I fear that we will be too late to homestead with them.

I leave the next few weeks in God's hands.

*****

Leah scrunched up the pillow under her neck and let her head loll back a bit. She took her hands and traced the outlines of her body prone on this bed on her back. A momentary vision of her in the same pose in a coffin assailed her. She tried to push it aside and then remembered when she had been in the Sherman Oaks bungalow, just seven and a half years old, doing the very same thing. She could hear her parents' strident voices from the kitchen breakfast nook, and although she was supposed to be asleep, the tenor of their argument disturbed her usual nighttime thoughts. She let her mind roam away from the stories about Guinevere and Lancelot in the book by her bed and imagined herself instead as lying in a glass coffin like Sleeping Beauty. She could picture her parents coming before her, lifting the lid, their tears splashing her quiet white face. Her mother would be calling her Angel, and Daddy would have to hold Mama's elbow tightly so she wouldn't faint. Leah would like to be able to see that, and then, just as her mother turned away, her head bent in its black veil, Leah would pop up and laugh, telling the assembled mourners that it was all a joke; she, little Queen Leah, was alive. She had just wanted to see if she would really be missed.

Now Leah felt the same impulse. This time, though, she wasn't testing the depth of grief of her family. She was taking a moment to remember what her friend Joanie had told her during a conversation shortly after the hepatitis diagnosis, about what it felt like to be single,

"Leah, honey," Joanie had said, not knowing that her friend had just that morning received the horrible news, "You can't take everyone with you. We all go into the earth alone. I don't think anyone's going to hold my hand and jump into the grave with me!"

Leah leaned across the lunch table at Le Central and took her friend's hand.

"I know all that. I just don't like to think about how alone we really are, you know? What does it all mean? Why do we get so connected, if we are ultimately by ourselves?"

"I don't know either, my friend, but I think maybe that's why we do connect. It's a way of staving off the inevitable, maybe." Joanie opened her purse to take out her lipstick and, while she applied creamy mauve color to her lips, searched Leah's face. "But what's up with this gloomy thinking? Oh, come on. Let's go to the movies. That way we can laugh at Woody's neuroses."

And they did just that.

Now, though, in this remote cabin, having sent away her anchor, Leah let herself wallow in premature grief for herself, maybe for her marriage, for all the lonely women in the world, for women of all time afraid to tell their husbands how they really felt.

Only when she heard a knock on the door and looked at the clock did she realize that she had drifted into a deep sleep that had lasted for several hours. The late afternoon sun slanted through the window as she arose to greet her visitor.

Chapter Sixteen

July 30

When she opened the door, the sight of Adam Caldwell, his tall figure filling the whole of her vision, made her fingers itch. She felt a rush of blood to her cheeks. She hadn't felt this way since the first time Ned had held her hand in the old Rialto Theater on Market Street as they watched Catherine Deneuve fall in love. Nonetheless, she let him in.

His arms were loaded with groceries, and he walked directly to the kitchen end of the main room.

"I hope this isn't too presumptuous, but I figured you might be eating alone, and I hoped you'd let me eat dinner with you."

He unloaded two big Idaho potatoes, a tri-tip roast, and fresh romaine lettuce, taking over the kitchen space just as he had done in the doorframe.

Leah joined him at the sink and let her mind wander to picturing him in other spaces. She occasionally checked out his smell, a mixture of mountain pine and aftershave, noticed the thick hair on his tanned arms as he rolled up the sleeves of his light flannel shirt, felt herself wanting to run her hands up his forearms, to feel the angle of that brown-blonde soft hair on her fingers, as she pressed it down, see it rise again as she moved on. She wanted the male warmth of his arms around her, she realized, and drew away slightly from him as he peppered the meat.

She set the table with her checkered place mats and bright red napkins, glad she had brought two sets, and then poured some wine from the bottle she and Ned had shared and sat down with him as they waited for the roast to cook. She couldn't help letting her imagination take over. What would he look like naked? Would he be as lean and hard as he appeared clothed? She had never touched his waist did he have a slight bulge of fat like Ned? He was certainly somewhere in his forties, she surmised, maybe a little older than she had thought at first. How many women had seen his body? She knew very little about him. Was he, perhaps, married? Had he ever been? He had never mentioned a significant other or children. Where had he lived before this?

Now she focused on his voice as he spoke of the day he'd spent hiking as far as he could climb. Was there a trace of accent? Leah couldn't detect anything eastern: no Boston "aa" or Chicago twang, no New Yawk r's. His voice was deep and resonant; it reminded her of the announcers she and Ned had worked with. Although she couldn't imagine that he had trained his speaking voice, nonetheless, she found herself mesmerized by its depth, its soothing quality.

"And that's why I want to go back to that peak," he was saying, as Leah arose and went to the kitchen to check the roast.

She returned with some crackers and bleu cheese she found in the refrigerator, again from Ned's visit. She handed him a cracker spread with the cheese, watched as he ate it. She studied his mouth. Wide and generous, she would describe it, the lips defined and not as full as they had felt on their first kiss. She wanted to feel them on hers again.

Instead, Leah moved a few inches farther from where she had been sitting just a few minutes ago and asked, "Adam. I was just thinking as you were talking. Do you have a regular home anywhere? I mean, are you going to be returning someplace in a few weeks?"

"That's odd…your asking, I guess. I thought I told you already. But then maybe I'm thinking about telling the realtor." Now Adam spread some cheese on a cracker and let her bite it from his hand. "I used to live in Seattle. But right now, I'm…well, you might say, feckless."

She tasted his fingers with her tongue. Clean but tart. *Did I just do that?* she thought.

"To tell you the truth," he continued, "I'm kind of living out of my car. The last couple of assignments and projects required travel anyway, and so I just decided to see how it felt to live without the usual anchors of home and hearth."

Anchors, that was a positive word to Leah. She rolled it around in her mind. She liked being anchored, loved her nest, her home, the butter-yellow cabinets of her kitchen, loved the idea of coming home to her sons and her regular life.

He continued, "As you know, I'm searching for a cabin around here, but I'm not even sure I want that. Afraid I'm a vagabond at heart."

Leah swallowed the rest of the cracker and looked at his coat and jacket thrown over the end of the sofa. She pictured him putting them on and taking them off, coming or going, a metaphor for the little she knew of him. He seemed always to be stopping by on the way to somewhere else. She suddenly had an image of him with children. It didn't fit.

"So," she looked him in the eyes, "no someone waiting for you anywhere, huh?" half hoping he'd say yes, so she could add that to her conscience's arsenal, yet half hoping he'd admit his availability.

"Nope. There was someone, but I said goodbye to that when I sold my home." When he didn't hear a response, he continued, "It's hard to explain, but I've made a conscious choice to try to simplify my life, to see how I can do without all the weight of things. That's my sense, anyway, gradually developed through the years of traveling and writing on the road, so to speak."

Leah traced her fingers along the cording of the rough sofa fabric, back and forth, while she studied the slope of his strong shoulders, noticed the muscles beneath his sleeves, then closely observed the way his clavicle began at the open neck of his shirt. Like a moth looking at a flame, she guessed.

"Don't you miss having a home?" she wondered aloud.

"Nope. Not so far. Oh, and by the way, in case you're wondering, I didn't leave anybody upset with me. I'm not on the lam. My girlfriend and I parted amicably. I don't even owe anyone any money." He smiled, waiting for her response.

"Any kids?" she said finally, voicing her unease. *If he had left lonely kids in Seattle, she'd shoot him.*

"Again, no. I decided about ten years ago when I was tempted with marriage that I'm not a kid type. I like children, but I'm too…" He searched for the word, "unattached, I guess. I just didn't think it fair to father children and then be gone all the time. My wanderlust exceeds my other lusts, I guess."

Leah felt a bittersweet something dropping within her that she couldn't analyze. She now knew she wasn't encroaching on another woman's territory and her flirtation would harm no children. None on his side, at least. As if on cue, she looked over at the photo of her boys.

She heard the timer and, with a sigh, got up from the sofa.

During dinner, she was spellbound by his tales of his travels. His world was exotic, as he had been on assignments in most of the continents of the world. He was relating his experience with a scholar in Benares, India, when Leah felt a piercing pain in her liver. He stopped and observed her carefully.

"Leah? You look ashen. What's the matter?"

"Nothing. Really. I just got full all of a sudden. Sorry." Leah looked down at her plate. The baked potato was uneaten, the slices of tri-tip still in their juices. All she could see was the half-nibbled salad of romaine leaves and fresh tomatoes. Adam had given her barely touched food the same once-over.

The ache returned, this time with more force.

"I'm sorry, Adam. I've got to go lie down. Please excuse me."

She felt dizzy as she got out of the chair and covered the few feet to the sofa without fainting.

Adam followed her and helped her, gently lifting her legs up to the pillows and removing her clogs. She closed her eyes and let the pain subside before asking him to bring her a glass of water and some of the Tylenol on the sink.

After Adam helped her lift her head and drink the water, he moved to the other end of the sofa and remained quiet for a few minutes.

"Leah? Would you like me to go?" Adam lifted his head and peered at her. Her eyes were open, and the color was returning to her cheeks.

"No. I'm better. Thanks, though. In fact, I'd like you to stay. I need to tell you something."

"OK. But first, maybe you'd feel better with some tea. I can fix it."

"Sure. There's some in that basket by the refrigerator. Would you like a cup, too?"

"Sounds good. I'll do it." And, as Adam filled the teapot, turned on the gas, found the cups in the cupboard, and sliced some lemon, Leah began her story. She started with the sliced wrist and told him as much as she could bear about the pain and the treatments and her prognosis.

By the time she was sitting upright, cradling the warm cup in her hands, letting the vapors of the herbal licorice tea mist her face, she could breathe and let her words to him sink in.

He settled next to her, drank deeply of his non-herbal brew, then put the cup down on the coffee table, and leaned in closer to her. He placed his arm behind her, and let his fingers massage her neck. Leah relaxed into the sensations supplanting her queasiness for two or three minutes, grateful for this respite.

"Balm in Gilead. It does exist. That feels wonderful," she said. "When I was a girl in Sunday school, we practiced singing spirituals for Easter, and that was one of them. I always wondered why Gilead was the place that offered balm. Never did look up the biblical allusion. But I guess it just means that if we wait long enough, we will be comforted. At least that's how I imagine the slaves who sang that song thought of heaven. Gilead. A place where they wouldn't suffer any more."

Leah stopped, aware that Adam hadn't interrupted her rush of words.

"I just wish now I could believe that there was a place for me like that. I wish I had that kind of faith. Is this too much for you to hear? I'm sorry."

"No, no, no. Leah. I'm listening. I'm trying to think of how you must feel." He paused. "To tell the truth, I was stalled at the point where you mentioned Sunday school. I could imagine you with a big blue bow in your hair, for some reason. I gather you're not as religious anymore."

"Not the way I thought I would be then. My mother and I went to that church for several months until I started having nightmares about her going to hell." Leah had an image of her mother throwing away cigarettes in the toilet before guests came to the door, fanning the air and popping a Sen-Sen.

"She drank martinis before dinner and sneaked cigarettes once in a while, and I thought from the preachers' sermons about sin that she would die in the night and be sent to fry because of her vices. We stopped going to that church, but I really think my mother actually thought her smoking was a sin. She finally quit, maybe about the time she stopped drinking."

Leah looked up at his face, aware again that she was giving him more information than he needed.

"But I rant on. I still have a sense of sin, you know. I remember when I was thirteen, and I'd met my first boyfriend at a matinee one Saturday afternoon in August. We had flirted with each other at the neighborhood pool and decided to meet during one of the Lone Ranger serials. We wound up kissing in the tenth row while my little brother crawled around under the seats driving everyone crazy. Later Davey, my brother, told my mom he'd seen me and Benny necking. I thought I'd die of humiliation.

"But the worst thing was that on Sunday of that same weekend, I went to church and the preacher gave a sermon I've never forgotten. He said that he wanted everyone to imagine that there was a huge TV screen set up right there in front of the congregation, and that God was recording our thoughts at that very moment for everyone else to see on the big screen. You can imagine that, at that exact second, I'd been thinking about Benny's kisses in the darkened theater, so I was sure that someone could indeed read my mind!

"My mother always said that morality was doing the right thing even when no one else could notice."

She stopped, watching him.

"So are you still a good girl?"

"Yes, actually. In some sense, I've always tried to heed Mom's advice, to remember that injunction. I think I've been a fairly moral and upright person. Except for a few Bennys in my wild youth."

Adam studied her arm, the delicate bone structure of her wrist.

"By the way, I have something I need to tell you, too, now that I know why you are up here so far from your family."

He paused to move closer to her, now taking his fingers away from her neck, moving his arm around down to her shoulder. He pulled her toward him and she leaned into his chest. She couldn't meet his eyes.

"When I met you at the real estate office, I thought you were about the most beautiful woman I'd ever seen. I saw your ring, but when I asked Betty about you, she said you were up here by yourself for a few weeks, didn't even hook up phone service. So a wishful side of me assumed that you were separated from your husband or up here to think things over. You know, about your marriage.

"Then I bumped into you fishing, and nothing you did contradicted my expectations. Anyway, I'm certainly not a sexual predator or someone who would want to seduce a married woman. I hope you know that."

Now Leah felt her heart pound. *Seduce? He used that word. There it was. Was she being seduced?* Deep inside she hoped so.

"I do think you are probably a pretty honorable guy. I really don't have much to go on, but you strike me as someone who's up front." She put down her tea, reached across, and touched his hand now resting on her arm. "Maybe it's the rugged outdoor look. Anyway, I am a responsible adult who can own up to my part in all of this." She looked around the cabin. "This. Your being here, my letting you kiss me the other night. I'm not thirteen and learning about boys for the first time."

"Well, then. Let me say it again. You are simply spectacularly gorgeous, and I'm smitten. Whatever is going on, I'm beyond acting responsibly."

He pulled away just far enough to be able to take her face in his hands. He leaned down and touched her lips lightly with his.

Leah felt herself stirring, felt sensations she had forgotten, but also had an unpleasant reminder of reality.

"Adam, wait. We need to stop for a minute. Just so you remember. I've got hepatitis C. I am feeling fine now—never better, but that means there is a risk with being physical with someone, though very slight. I've never had to say this before—"

Adam interrupted, "So I need to have protection, is that what you're saying?"

"Yes. This just sounds so clinical, but I guess that's the way it is. I'm in unfamiliar territory. I mean, Ned knows me and my illness, but here I am having to bring up all this... stuff. I'm sorry."

"Oh, Leah. You are so dear." Adam took her chin in his hand now and gazed at her eyes. "A vagabond is always prepared. I have condoms in my wallet. That's just the way the world is nowadays. I'm a mature man living an unattached life. So of course, I'm ready for any eventuality, including you. Oh...and, by the way, you are just about the best thing I could ever imagine being prepared for."

He had put her at ease, and again he leaned down and kissed her, this time more ardently than before. She knew they had crossed over into some experience she could not rescind, even if she wanted to. To be desired by a man who thought she was beautiful had almost become an alien concept. It seemed so long ago, so far in the past, that even her husband had told her that she was lovely. But this man here, this minute, wanted her. *Comfort her. Balm in Gilead.*

Chapter Seventeen

August 15, 1863

Thaddeus is healing—his leg is stronger each day—but he is increasingly irritable as he wrestles over our change in plans. I am making myself useful in many ways at Fort Boise while he recuperates. The men stationed here say that my hours in the kitchen are a source of joy; the food that I help cook reminds them of home. I must say that I can't notice any flavors. I am still not very interested in eating, and yet my weight is increasing.

I did finally tell Thaddeus this week about the life within me. I had hoped he would be more excited than he appeared to be, but I suppose that has more to do with girlish dreams than with the realities of his increased responsibilities as we face an uncertain future. The most recent wagon train to stop here at the fort left yesterday. These pioneers were also beset by many problems on their trek and are at least three weeks behind schedule. They indicated that they were probably the last train to be on the route this year. They had even been passed by a train that took the Pacific Springs turn off to California several weeks back when they had stopped, as we had, for wagon repairs.

The travelers all spoke of a sense of urgency, of pressure to hurry up and get back on the trail to Oregon. They are afraid that they will miss the chance to homestead and get some temporary shelter before it gets bitter cold.

After they left and I waved my kerchief goodbye to the final wagon, I went to Thaddeus and expressed my fears. I had not wanted to burden him with my doubts, and I do know he has been in many discussions with the staff here at the fort about our options, but I was not prepared for his latest thoughts on our plight.

"Linnea," he said, when I pulled up a chair next to his cot, "I've decided that we should abandon our plans to continue on to Oregon."

When I gasped, he continued.

"Dr. Barrett has told me that I must remain bedridden for another month. That means that it will be too late for us to rejoin any caravan this year. Even if we should somehow be able to go on by ourselves, we won't get to our destination until November, probably, and then what can we do?"

I responded, in great anguish for both of us, but especially for Thaddeus, who has held firm to this dream for many months, "Then what else is possible?"

He took my hand and watched me carefully for my reaction as he spoke.

"I have given this great thought. As soon as I am ready, I will take a horse up north of here along a small trail along the river. Apparently, there are gold mines and a burst of activity along the sides of that river and I will search for some lodging we may use during the winter months. It may even be that we can benefit from some of the sudden wealth that I am told is being made from the rich lodes of ore there. Then we can decide what we wish to do next spring after the baby is born."

I can hardly relate what fear I feel as I think of our predicament, but I trust my husband to make the right decision. He found out about a land office here in Boise and understands that the same offer of 160 acres is available in Idaho Territory. According to Thaddeus, we will be able to take advantage of that offer near our next stop. Although I wouldn't say this to him, I feel that we will be cast adrift up there instead of in Oregon Territory. At least, we would have been within riding distance of people we knew from the wagon train, near friends with similar experiences. But to be in the midst of miners? It doesn't sound right to me, but as ever I shall accede to my husband's will.

September 16, 1863

I have just waved goodbye to my husband as he left on his explorations North. I am fearful that he is not recovered well enough to take this journey, but he insists. Dr. Barrett has reluctantly given his approval to the long ride, but I am sure that he was persuaded by the chill in the air even as I write this. Thaddeus should be able to reach the area of mines in several days, especially as he is traveling alone and can move faster that way.

While he is gone, I will continue my efforts to consolidate our dwindling possessions. If we do decide to settle some place north of here, I shall take only minimal items with me. We will not have time to outfit our larger wagon, nor am I sure it will make the journey north, but the fine gentlemen here at the fort have said that we can store our bulkier items with them. Nonetheless, I do not look forward to such uncertainty. I will just have to trust that all of this change has been preordained and is meant to lead to a more positive outcome. I think often of our companions of the Oregon Trail. By now, they must have reached their homesteading land. I am sure it is the cause of celebration and joy and trust that they are all well.

I have sent many letters from here to Ingrid. My greatest wish is that she may eventually join us wherever we are. I wish I could talk with her now about the movement I feel inside me. I felt a wee kick the other day. These slight flutters give

*me the energy and faith to believe that God has a plan for our
little family.*

*****

August 2, 1998

Leah put the diary down for a few minutes. She was outside the cabin by the bank of flowers she had planted when
she first arrived. Now, just a few weeks later, she was able to
admire the burst of blossoms and hues of blue, yellow, and
red. She could smell the tangy odor of the marigolds edging
the flowerbed; at this precise moment, her life felt full. Her
great-great-grandmother's youth and tenuous future jumped
out in spite of the delicate penmanship. She had, after all,
only been twenty-three when she wrote these lines. Leah
could imagine herself pregnant, alone in new territory, facing
a radical change of plans.

She knew Linnea had no choice but to accept the designs
of her husband. The fact that she had related his proposals
with such equanimity was what amazed her.

Leah, too, had an uncertain future ahead of her, but
she, at least, could have some impact on the outcome. It was
finally her decision whether she embarked on a new round of
Interferon therapy, whether she continued her dalliance with
Adam, or whether she grabbed life's many possibilities with
an eye only to her own health or with the responsibility she
had been given to be a wife and mother.

Leah allowed thoughts of Adam to enter her consciousness, trying to understand the mixture of emotions she felt
for him. She couldn't simply put away the feelings he had

rekindled in her just two nights ago when they had made love. And yet there were other issues to examine.

What had surprised Leah most, as she clasped Adam's firm chest to her heart and stroked his back after they had both fallen inert from the force of their ardor, was that the one emotion she had expected and didn't feel was guilt! She hadn't even compared this relative stranger to the man she had held so many times over the years of her maturity. The thought of Ned only came once, at the realization that she wasn't thinking of him, then, of course, that meant she was.

Adam had risen from the bed sometime during the middle of the night, and she had awakened to a mild sense of disorientation. Where his long body had been, there was only the cool sheet. Before she drifted into sleep, she felt his legs entwined in hers but hadn't even noticed him slip away.

It had been two days now, and while Leah hadn't been assailed by remorse, she also hadn't missed Adam as intensely as she might have thought. The minute she had taken off her clothes, exposing herself entirely to his gaze, she believed she had entered some new territory that would change her forever. How, after all, could she even entertain the idea of loving someone other than Ned unless it was the kind of dramatic life-changing passion from which she would never be able to recover? The only thing worth violating her marriage vows for must, by definition, be overwhelming.

She had certainly felt sexual passion when she was with Adam, but it seemed now to be in perspective. As Leah sat here near the warm Idaho earth and under the shade of her favorite aspen, she noted only that she felt relatively passive. The memory of two nights ago was lovely but not one needing urgent response, a re-planning of her life.

Leah had known women who could have casual sexual encounters. She had never imagined that she would be one of them. But today, she had to look clearly at her emotions. How could she be so, well, blasé concerning that gorgeous man she had caressed so fervently? In retrospect, Adam seemed more like a figment of her imagination than the real person who had touched her deeply. It was as though he had flitted into her space for a brief but intense period and then was gone, like the hummingbirds that visited her. At this very instant, a magnificent blue butterfly was adoring the flower it rested upon. Neither would ever be exactly the same when the butterfly flew away, the flower touched by the beauty of the creature who had borrowed it for a few seconds, the flier intent upon flying toward new beauty. Life itself, her life, even, was transitory.

She picked up the pages of scientific studies she had been reading in between Linnea's diary accounts. She had pored over anecdotal information about the ravages and successes of Interferon. She knew what the treatments were like: she hardly needed to be told about other's experiences. She closed her eyes and let everything just seep in, fill her for a few minutes. Statistics, the feel of Adam's hands on her hips, the subtext of her forebear's stoic resignation, all lapped over each other and, in a montage of images, Leah sank into her own dilemma, her family filling her recollections.

*****

"Mom? Mom? Where are you? Mom?"

The voice was clearer as Tim figured out that his mother wasn't downstairs and started up the flight of steps to his parents' bedroom.

Leah stirred in her stupor, the sleep finally induced by painkillers taken this morning. She rolled her head to her right, straining to see the time on the antique alarm clock. Four o'clock. *Four o'clock in the afternoon?* Leah had no sense of time. With the blinds closed, the light was indeterminate. The only clue to validate her senses was the voice of her son, now at the bedroom door.

"Mom? Can I come in?" A pause. "Mom? It's Tim."

Leah rose up a bit on her elbow, exhaustion making the action difficult. "Sure, honey. Come on in."

When Tim entered, she had closed her eyes to ward off the queasy feeling. She kept them closed but motioned to him with the arm outside her comforter.

"Hi, honey. Come here. Sit by the side of the bed. I'm OK. Just resting my eyes for a bit." She patted Ned's side of the bed.

She felt the slight weight of his thin body on the edge of the bed. She waited for him to speak.

"Mom? Are you sure? I can come back later."

"Of course I'm sure. What's up?" Leah squinted her eyes open enough to locate his hand, the one he was leaning on. She put hers on his.

"Nothing much. I just wanted to see how you are. Oh, and also, to tell you I got really good grades. They're being mailed home today, but my teachers let us know in class."

Tim had recently completed his first semester at middle school as she had just begun her new life as an Interferon subject. She didn't think she could absorb the juxtaposition of those two realities, but she mustered up the energy to give him a smile and pat his hand.

"Oh, honey. I'm so glad. I'll be excited to get them in the mail." She looked closer at her gangly son. He was a little too thin, his flesh stretched over his long bones, though she could sense in him for the first time the handsome man he would become. She saw his features filled out, his shoulders broadened, and smiled again as she imagined him wowing the girls in a few fleeting years.

"Let's talk more about it later when your dad gets home. Where's Jeff?" Leah realized that she hadn't heard his usual after-school thumping of the basketball on the driveway court.

"Mom, don't you remember? He's spending the night at Johnny's. Johnny's mom said if there was any way she could help, she would, and you and Dad decided that it would be good to have him away for a couple of days. So that's where he is."

"Oh, sure, I remember. I'm sorry, honey. I'm just a little cloudy right this minute. What's for dinner?"

As Tim started to tell her of Ned's arrangements, Leah felt herself pass again into the semi-consciousness of drugs. She found herself straining to keep awake, to keep contact with her son as he tried to assure her that they would be fine.

We'll be fine, she thought, as she blacked out.

But they weren't really fine ever again. In the year and a half since that first treatment, Leah had experienced many days like that one, whole chunks of time she wanted to be with her boys eclipsed by the ravages caused by pain or the numbness to deal with it.

Before she agreed to undergo Interferon, she had understood that it was often a drastic experiment and that she would experience pain and fatigue, but she had not considered the toll it would take on the rest of her family. How could she have known? How could she have predicted that her days and nights and almost every activity over the last eighteen months would be determined by her reactions to the drug or the tests which informed her of the treatment results? How could she have known that every single activity in her family would be predicated by the word *if*? "*If* Mother's up to it, we can…" "*If*

115

Leah's strong enough, we'd love to…" or "Your mother wants to see the game. "*If* she can, she will come." They planned their lives around her shots.

How could she have known that the pattern of their days would be determined by terms such as "millions of units" to take down viral levels also stated in millions? These were concepts she could barely comprehend, much less associate with her body.

Of course, as any person might imagine, Leah thought she would be the subject who would show up in the exceptional column; she would be among the few who flourished under this regimen, that she wouldn't experience the side effects, that yes, there would be discomfort, but that her positive outlook and naturally optimistic disposition would enable her to triumph over the negatives and prove the dry scientists wrong. Those are the images we have of ourselves, she knew. For years, she had mildly ascribed to the concept that people were responsible for their own health. She had joined others of her generation who blithely said cancer was caused by stress or bad living for, after all, if one could employ good eating habits and a wholesome lifestyle toward good health, then it stood to reason that bad health was also one's responsibility or fault.

This theory, however, didn't explain the child who died or the random incidences of rare disease or the premature deaths of friends she had loved.

In Sherman Oaks, Leah had a bubbly and happy little friend in first grade who didn't show up one day to school. Two weeks later, when she learned that Annabelle had died, Leah insisted on knowing the details. While her mother tried to soften the news, she was of a generation that believed in not shielding children from reality, and so she explained to Leah the nature of Annabelle's death.

Even now, after dozens of years and having read up on the illness, Leah could not rid her mind of the picture she had formed of her friend Annabelle curled up in agony from spinal meningitis. Somewhere, she had heard someone whisper about the strange position and curvature of the child's spine and the oddly-shaped coffin. Leah often wondered if the coffin part was true, but nonetheless, the image haunted her.

Surely, Annabelle hadn't done anything to deserve this disease.

Neither had Leah, she finally decided after months of anguish. A mysterious virus had entered her blood through a fluke, an accidental transfer of the disease, even before there was the ability to properly screen blood for this form of hepatitis. The only thing she had done wrong was to try to stuff a bulky styrofoam dish into a trash compactor. If that made her responsible, she was paying a terrible price for a stupid mistake.

That first morning, after the initial injection of Interferon, had indeed been a signal of the rest to come. Actually, Leah felt grateful to have survived the night. When Dr. Cantrell had told her she would need injections of three million units of the drug three times a week for about six months, she had recoiled. But since it seemed to be the only hope for her particular combination of symptoms, she had just gritted her teeth and jumped into the preparations. She and Ned learned how to administer the injections themselves, on Mondays, Wednesdays, and Fridays, with two days off each weekend. The previous night, Ned had given her the first injection and then lay down beside her to help her through the ordeal. Neither of them had been prepared for what happened.

It was like being poisoned. First, Leah began shaking. She shook so that the bed actually bounced, and as Ned tried to hold her steady, she was wracked by deep bone aches, aches to the core, chills and flashes of heat intermingled. One symptom would subside and another would take hold. She spent six hours in this manner before she gave into the medicines that were to be taken only if the pain became unbearable. Ned finally grabbed a couple of hours of sleep before getting Tim ready for school and going to work, and in utter exhaustion, Leah fell asleep. This was the state in which Tim had found her.

And while her body learned to tolerate the treatments a little better as time wore on, Leah lived between injections with the nightmare of dread so that even her painless days were consumed by mental preparation for the next dose of the drug. For six months, Leah lived a life on the edge of exhaustion and fear.

She had dealt with many other consequences of the regimen. She proved to be. indeed, typical of most other Interferon users, not the exception. Although she didn't lose much of her hair, she had funny clumps of small bald spots, she cried easily, she developed a foggy brain, and she became depressed, a state she likened to continuous PMS. She lost her capacity to feel; not only had she felt little passion for Ned in terms of their sex life, but she felt generally passionless about everything else. She seemed numb to events around her. She could hardly stomach reading *The Chronicle* or discussing the news with friends. She simply didn't relate to much beyond her interior life.

Worse than all of these, however, was the loss she felt about her sons. It had taken one year for her to get her energy back, to feel like going to work with Ned or fixing meals for her men; a year during which Tim had his first crush on a girl, something Ned told her about months after it was over; a year when Jeff pitched an almost perfect Little League regional semi-finals game while she was at home throwing up in the toilet; a year when she was too weak to attend parent conferences—she'd never even met the teacher who took Miss Rose's place when she ran off to get married; a year where Jeff grew two inches and developed a stutter; a year lost to her forever.

And the final irony: the treatments had been unsuccessful, and now Dr. Cantrell was urging her to begin a new series of Interferon treatments combined with Riboviron, in a dosage of six million units three times a week, to begin again the process of hope while the virus multiplied in her bloodstream, out of control.

Could she once again subject her family to this?

Chapter Eighteen

October 23, 1863

I am sitting in a dark little room upstairs in a small hotel called Miners' Rest. It is 6:00 at night, and I have just finished our first supper with the hotel's owners, Bethanne and Tom Murphy. I feel as though I am adrift. Our room is sparse but adequate, with log walls and two small windows. Thaddeus and I will share a rough-hewn wood bed. I have put mother's quilt on it to help it seem like home. Next to it is the desk whereat I sit writing by the light of a kerosene lamp. As I look out the small window above the desk, all I see are stands of trees. It is still light out, though the evenings are coming sooner after the summer of late sunsets. It is cold and the air is crisp. Some of it seems to leak in through the logs, so I have put on two sweaters. I can hear the river rushing nearby.

I am still amazed at the turn of events that has brought us to this isolation. When Thaddeus returned with news that there was a place we could stay for the winter, I readily acceded to his plans. I really had no choice, come to think of it. Thaddeus has said that we will only be here for the winter and that we can resume our plans for homesteading at springtime when the snows melt and the baby is born. While I would have preferred to stay on at Fort Boise, Thaddeus wouldn't stand for it. He's really not very fond of the military, and if truth were told, he has a spirit of adventure which makes him restless. I wonder if he will always *seek something around the corner instead of accepting what we have.*

So two weeks ago, we piled a few possessions into packs and satchels and set off by horseback and mule for this new place. We have been lucky with the weather, and the first few days were actually rather hot and easy for travel. Then we arrived at the river which I can hear rushing now, and our travel became more hazardous. I admit to some discomfort because of my pregnancy, but Thaddeus was considerate in not trying to cover too many miles each day. I had time to rest in between our periods of riding.

We encountered others on the trail, mostly miners who had heard about the discovery of rich lodes in the mountains along this river. They have the same destination as we do but a very different goal: they are possessed of frenzy for the acquisition of gold. I have been able to ascertain that some are veterans of long years in California trying to find the gold that was so prevalent there this past decade. Many are thin and bitter and tell stories about greed and disappointment that are alien to my concept of life's values.

I am especially aware that there are few women on the trail. I fear living in a place, even for a short while, that lacks the softening presence of women. Thaddeus tells me that more women will come to Miner's Rest after the men settle in, but he and I both know that most of these women will be women of easy virtue, brought to mining towns to satisfy the needs of lonely men. I am filled with trepidation.

Bethanne, thank goodness, seems like a good woman. She is heavy-set, with thick, wiry reddish-brown hair that she wears in braids. She has a full figure and a maternal quality. She greeted me with a firm hug and fed us a good stew as soon as we sat down. I think I am fortunate to have an ally here. I have prom-ised to help her as much as I can with cooking and cleaning in exchange for our room and board here through the winter. Thaddeus is planning on working in the claims office next door.

Thus, I face my first night at the beginning of yet another new set of experiences. I will pray for the strength I need, even as I feel my child within kicking and shifting. At least I have Thaddeus to hold in the long hours until dawn.

*****

October 30

My days here have settled into a routine and I feel blessed. Every morning I arise early to help Beth with preparations for breakfast. We usually feed about twenty-five men staying here until they decide their next steps. Thaddeus rises with them and then goes to the nook he calls an office; it is really just the size of a large outhouse equipped with a safe, a small desk and a window he can push up when he opens for business. He is busier than he thought he would be because there are so many new miners coming by each day to stake a claim on one of the veins in these hills. Thaddeus is learning a great deal about the law as he tries to assess the fairness of each claim, and he proceeds with caution with each encounter.

Usually in the morning, I wash clothes or iron for Beth. Until my arrival, I doubt she ever had a spare minute! As it is, we work all day cleaning, cooking, and sometimes even settling an argument among the residents. Beth is stronger than I could have imagined. One look from her formidable brow and most of the men retreat from their positions. Sometimes, emotions run high, though, and it makes me appreciate the laws we lived by in Massachusetts. Her husband, John, has had to use his rifle more than once to ensure the departure of an unruly guest.

Beth listens to my yearnings in a way I realized I have missed since Helen and I used to talk with each other on the trail. A good woman friend seems to be one of the necessities of life, indeed. I have learned things about her life which give me courage. She and John were innkeepers in Kansas for about ten years before he caught the Go-West disease. It took them another two years to arrive at this spot, where they have been since the first whisperings about gold and silver.

There are some other women in town, of course. As I predicted, many are women of easy virtue. They remain most of the time within the walls of their residence, which is located five small shops away from our hotel. Once in a while, I spy one of them during the late afternoon before the men return from the fields, but they seem to prefer staying indoors. Yesterday, I was dusting one of the bedrooms when I heard a cry. I rushed to the window and saw a young girl being pulled by her ear by an older woman. Upon closer inspection, the girl couldn't have been more than fifteen or sixteen, but she already had blackened teeth and signs of wear on her tired face. The other woman was corpulent, with brassy dyed hair and traces of bruises on her face. I can't imagine what their argument was, but they soon disappeared from my view. As it was, I was spying, so I closed the window and went back to my chores.

Later I asked Beth about the women. She said that they were just poor whores. Poor whores. I am growing fonder of Beth each day, but her dismissal of these women strikes me as unkind. Just as I am stuck out here for the love of a man, so might they have taken a turn in their lives that made them victims of the whims of someone stronger than they. I actually don't feel much different, in a way. My life has been changed in ways I never would have predicted because of my love for Thaddeus. And now I find that Thaddeus and I are distanced from each other. We seem less and less close.

I miss him. Tonight, after I had cleaned up from supper, I found Thaddeus sitting in the entry room with some new arrivals. They were two men without women (both had lost them to early death) who had given up on homesteading and were going to try their luck at mining the lodes of Idaho Territory, I went over to Thaddeus, waited for a decent time to interrupt, and asked him to please come up to the room. I had something I wanted to speak with him about. Usually I am asleep by the time he comes to bed, and so I wanted him to know it was important.

When there was a pause in the conversation, I leaned down and whispered to him, "Thaddeus, dear, please come up to the room soon. I need to talk with you."

He took my hand from his shoulder, and I thought for a moment that he would keep it in his. Instead, he flung it aside and said, loudly enough for all in the room to hear, "Excuse me, gentlemen. My wife is being demanding, as usual."

He snorted with laughter and the men gave him what could only be termed commiserating glances.

Then he turned his face to me with the most horrible look and said, "Now, dear. We are discussing important things. I'll be up later."

I left, my cheeks flushing with humiliation and what I now recognize as rage, and scurried like a humble, good little mouse-wife, up to my room.

Perhaps I shouldn't have recorded this incident, but it is part of what this wilderness is doing to us, I fear.

*****

Linnea's thoughts:
(I don't understand where the Thaddeus I fell in love with has gone. Instead, I see this pompous man, whose belly

is getting paunchy, acting in a way that is foreign to what I thought was my understanding of his sweet nature. I am waiting here for his return. I don't like the feelings that this incident has stirred up in me. I especially don't like being angry and knowing there is little I can do with it. I am more afraid than ever of his rejection. I know I depend entirely upon him. I don't want to anger him, and I know I must be humble; it is my wifely responsibility. But oh, there are times when I would like to take my fists and pummel his back. I feel very un-Christian and know I must pray over this for the sake of my marriage and, more importantly, for my child.

I am still waiting for his tread on the steps but am so exhausted with labor and emotion that I may just have to sleep before it is settled. Where is he, the Thaddeus I love?)

*****

Leah closed the diary and walked to the table where she kept her CD player. From the pile of CDs she'd packed, she found one by The Platters, inserted it in the player, and let the sounds of "Only You" wash over her. Every time she heard this song, she was able to recall the intoxication of dancing with Ned.

One foggy night shortly after they purchased their house in Sausalito, they hosted a small celebratory dinner party, and somehow the conversation had shifted from politics to rock and roll, in a logical Bay Area connection.

Ned had arisen from dessert, gone over to the stereo, and put on the Beatles, the Platters and Jefferson Airplane, and the rest of the evening had been spent to the accompaniment of the sounds of the '60s and '70s. She and Ned finally rolled up the area rug and, with the sparkle of Tiburon's lights shining intermittently through the fog, started dancing.

When "Only You" came on, Leah locked her eyes with the deep blue of her husband's and sang along. What intensity, what absolute and supposedly undying love she had felt that evening! Even now, the back of her neck tingled at the recollection.

If she felt this now about Ned, how could she have even entertained a flirtation with Adam? Was it just that long-dormant sexual feelings had arisen in her isolation and at the flattering attentions of a new man? She pressed the CD controls and replayed "Only You," swaying slightly to the hypnotic voices and mellow rhythm of the music.

Chapter Nineteen

August 5, 1998

"N ed? Hi, It's me. I hope I'm not calling too late."

"Oh. No. Of course not. What's up?"

"I think I'm about ready to make some decisions. Just wanted to run my ideas by you. OK?"

Leah was surprised at the trepidation she felt, as though she was imposing on him—probably more to do with her feeling undeserving of his attention than due to anything he had done.

This afternoon, she had opened the rusty mailbox at the end of the driveway. She had been checking it every day, finding yellowed flyers and throwaway newspapers the first time she pulled down the door shaped like the heel of a loaf of bread. She hadn't expected anything, really, but her last letter to the boys was sent in an envelope on which she had clearly printed the Idaho address, and she had been nursing the faint hope that they would write her.

Today, she had been lucky, finding a misshapen envelope addressed to her in Tim's bold slant. When she turned it over, she found SWAK on the flap. It had been years since either of her boys had expressed such a mushy sentiment, and she was still smiling when she pulled up her chair under the tree next to the purple columbine and opened the letter. Out fell several blue ribbons, the reason for the envelope's bulk. They were encased in a rubber band with a small note tucked in. "Mom. These are for you. I've been winning lots of riding events the past couple of weeks. I've decided I want a horse." Then two big question marks and "Love you, Jeff."

She put the ribbons under the deck chair and unfolded Tim's two-page letter.

Dear Mom:

You know how hard it is for me and Jeff to admit it when you are right, but you are now. I was really mad at Sam Brunner when he separated the two of us, but it turns out that Jeff was forced to get some new friends. One of them is a kid who lives on a farm in Oregon and rides all the time. As you can see from the blue ribbons, he and Jeff have spent most of their time riding, and Jeff has gotten really good at it. I get to see him a lot because I spend so much time at the stables. So it's cool.

Last night, Jeff came over to my cabin. We decided to go and sit outside and look at the sky, just like you said in your last letter. We tried to imagine which stars you had named for us. We know which one we've named for you. It's the only one we can always pick out for sure and it always seems to be there, which is why we decided to call the North Star "Mom." So we hope you like that we did this.

We are getting a little bored with the food. Can you believe that we're getting tired of pancakes every day? Seriously, we can't wait for some of your own San Francisco cooking! Even your healthy food sounds good after so much spaghetti and macaroni and cheese.

I've probably gained six or seven pounds, but Jeff seems even thinner. I bet he's grown an inch or two.

I just wanted you to know that we are fine and happy but will be glad to get home in a couple of weeks.

And, Mom, whatever you decide is OK with us.

Leah blinked back tears before finishing the letter.

We love you and know that whatever you and Dad do will be the right thing.

Love, Tim.

Leah put down the pages and, shielding her eyes from the suddenly too-bright morning sun, let her head ret on the back of the chair until she could open her eyes again. Where had this almost grown-up young man come from? She had said goodbye earlier this summer to her boys, and one of them had been becoming an adult without letting her in on it. Tim's letter, with its mature and honest attitudes and (with pride, she realized) good language skills, "blew her away," as Jeff would put it. Had she missed something? Or had she just not been with him at one of those exact moments in life when you can almost see a transition, some action or behavior that signals a new phase of existence? On the other hand, perhaps she was witnessing it in this letter. For her baby was now a young man.

Now she asked Ned, "Have you talked with the boys recently?"

"Sure. They're fine." Ned waited for more.

"Well, I got a letter from them this morning. Oh, Ned, it was wonderful! I just wanted to check in and see if I was simply imagining it or if they were trying to fool me. But I think they sound like they are having a wonderful time. Do you agree?"

"Sure do. And I actually talked with Jeff on the phone a couple of days ago. He's very caught up in riding this year."

Leah laughed. "Is he subtly letting you know that he wants a horse?"

"But of course," Ned replied. "He wouldn't be our son if he didn't start lobbying as soon as he knows he wants something."

Leah reflected for a few seconds on the irony of that statement. Come to think of it, both she and Ned were very forthright in stating their wishes. She just wished she could be more certain of hers.

"Listen, Ned. I've done my reading. I don't like the prospect, but I think maybe when I return, I'll prepare to do it. I'll do the Interferon, the supposedly improved one with the other factors that Dr. Cantrell recommends."

Ned sighed audibly. "Oh, honey. I'd hoped for this. I just don't want to see any more damage to your liver." He paused just a beat or two. "But then, I'm not the one who has to suffer as I saw you suffer these past months."

Leah thought, *Butterfly kisses, long nights.* "Look, Ned. I'm not absolutely sure about all of this, but what I really want to know before I make the call is how you think the boys will do if I'm out of commission again for so long."

"Lee, you know they'll do anything they can to get you through it. They understand that you're the kind of mother who would go through any pain, do anything, whatever, if you could possibly be with them. Of course, they want you cured. I think they understand completely."

Now his voice took on a deeper and more modulated tone. "And anyway, what other options are there? Do we just wait around until medical science comes up with a better treatment in the next few years? In the meantime, your liver may sustain irreparable damage. So what other choices do we have?"

Leah had to choose her words carefully.

"At least, with these attempts, I can believe that I'm staving off the inevitable—maybe long enough for something better to be developed." There, she had said it. *The inevitable. What was that really? Death? We all die.* She just didn't want what time she had left to be spent trying to delay a process that might come sooner than she wished anyway, and in the meantime taking away all the precious things she could do with her sons. What was so baffling about this illness was that people afflicted with it often had varied symptoms and levels of discomfort, and even she could experience this treatment differently than she had before. She wanted to avoid further damage to her liver with the resulting cirrhosis and failure to function. She had met others with her disease who were now awaiting liver transplants. It could get a lot worse if she didn't take measures to slow, if not halt, the disease's progress.

Would she be in bed in pain in a darkened room the first time she might see her son's face light up at the sight of a girlfriend? How many plays or debate tournaments would she miss? Would she ever be able to watch Jeff show off his new riding skills? Not if she were pinned down by pain and nausea as she had been during her last cycle of treatments.

On the other hand, maybe paying for some of the lost times now would later yield the rewards of a prolonged life or even a cure. One hoped for new solutions, new drug discoveries. Maybe missing a soccer match now would mean she could see her sons married and hold her first grandchild in her arms.

In her research, she had come up with the daunting figure that perhaps less that 20 percent of hepatitis C subjects who tried Interferon saw any long-lasting change for the better. Not good odds. On the other hand, the last time she had been tested, her viral levels had doubled to twenty-five million units, so time was rushing ahead.

Ned interrupted her thoughts. "Well, darling, you know I'll live with whatever you think is best. So just decide and let me know. By the way, when are you coming back? It's been so long, and the boys will be home soon. We all want you here if possible."

"I know. I'm getting ready. I promise. Probably just a few more days."

"OK. Whatever you want."

Ned sounded resigned, but Leah also noted that he hadn't pulled out his full sales pitch or tried to pressure her the way he used to. She knew he spent hours on the Internet researching new approaches to her illness. Mr. Fixit was OK. She felt relief and gratitude.

"Thanks, Ned. I'll call you in a few days. If you talk to the boys, tell them I got their wonderful letter and, of course, that I love them."

"Sure. And remember that we love you. Be safe and careful."

Leah's throat constricted.

"Me, too," she said. "Bye," and turned off the phone.

Chapter Twenty

August 7, 1998

Now she understood the frustrations of fishing. She had chosen this spot because she'd been here before and thought she could read its contours, the places where the brush hung low enough to cover the edges of the creek and provide shelter for the trout swimming beneath. She had walked its banks several times, noting that even where it widened, the brush grew right to the water. It was an ideal habitat. And she had seen a hatch just downstream the other day. This could be the spot where she'd have some success. She knew enough from her father and then her lessons to take the water temperature; at 57 degrees, it was a little on the cold edge of acceptable but nonetheless should have been good for the fish she knew were there.

Earlier, she had tried grasshopper imitations to no avail. Since it was midsummer and she had observed many terrestrial insects flirting with the water, now she tied on one of her father's mayfly flies. She saw how carefully the speckled wings and dark bands on the dry fly imitated so closely the actual markings of the mayflies she had seen darting near the water. As she attached it, she could almost feel her father's hands instructing her in the correct knots, his strong chest behind her, his arms enfolding her while he took her through the delicate maneuvers. Odd, how some small things stayed with one long after other more important events disappeared from memory. She could recreate that clinch knot immediately the first time she tried it after so many years, but she couldn't recall the sound of her father's voice.

She saw some concentric rings by the west bank and cast her line just upstream. She congratulated herself on how it hit the correct spot the first time. She watched the direction of the current, waited for the rise of a fish, then tried again several times, each cast more hypnotic as she was forced to concentrate on its rhythm and destination. She loved this, felt her nagging rush to make personal decisions fade away as she continued her quest for the elusive trout.

She had an understanding why men dominated this sport. Perhaps, she mused, it was because they could get away during the hours women needed to cook breakfast or dinner, even in mountain retreats or simply because it did provide such a relief from the tensions of making a living. She also considered a sneaky notion that it fit the male need for leisure activity that had a practical end, something concrete that could be accomplished, like woodworking, repairing cars, or finding a problem to solve. At any rate, she was glad her father had introduced her to the mysteries of fishing.

Finally, as the sun went down behind the large trees lining both sides of the water, she climbed up the slope of the shore, removed her waders, and pulled on her tennis shoes. She wiped and separated the parts of her father's old bamboo rod and removed the delicate fly. As she tucked it into its corner of the tackle box and closed the clasp, Leah experienced a tingle down her spine. She realized now that she had been waiting all evening for the telltale snap of a twig, a signal that Adam might be near. Now that it was dusk, she had resigned herself to his absence. Surely, since it had been three days since she had seen him, he would want to come by, to check up on her, at least, to let her know that their night together had lingered in his thoughts as well as hers.

She recalled a joke one of her divorced friends had told her after not hearing from a man she had dated. At the time, it had seemed grossly funny although certainly politically incorrect. A woman on safari in Africa is raped by a huge orangutan and kept captive by him for two days and nights. Several months later, as she relates the incident to her psychiatrist, she bursts into tears. The doctor attempts to soothe her, giving her Kleenex and assuring her that, with intensive therapy, the ordeal can be put into perspective.

"But, Doctor," she cries, "You don't understand. He hasn't even called!"

Ruefully, she understood the meaning behind the joke. Most women want follow-up. She stilled herself, waiting for the footsteps she sensed were near, but when none came, she arose, brushed the pine needles off her jeans, and put on her jacket. It was getting cold as the sun slipped further down behind the mountain peak.

Now another twig cracked as something bent it. This time, Leah's shiver was one of dread. Adam would have identified himself by now. She decided to start walking away from the sound, as though she hadn't heard it, so she picked up her gear, turned her back to the known path, and headed up the slight slope away from the stream.

Again, she heard the rustle of branches and leaves.

"Adam?" she called, thinking he might be testing her with his quiet presence. "Adam?"

She kept on moving. About fifty feet from the spot she'd been fishing, she turned right, into a thicket of brush she sensed might have a way out on the other side. As she felt the sharp twigs sting her face, she veered left a bit and encountered something solid and warm. She recoiled, but huge flannel-clad arms grabbed her and stopped her.

She gasped. She knew it wasn't Adam. She could smell a thick odor of alcohol, the rancid stink of body odor, and a musty something from the beard which now brushed against her forehead. She closed her eyes; she didn't want to see the rest of the person holding her so tightly. Her heart was pounding, and she felt her lips drying up as she tried to still the panic rising within her, tasting the bile in her mouth.

"Please. Let me go."

The man held her tighter.

"Please. Whoever you are. Let me go."

She turned her face up now, looking at the man so close to her. Certainly not Adam! Instead, the person resembled her stereotype of a mountain man, the cliché represented by one of those carved wooden figures sold at curio shops along California's Highway 49. He was classically grizzled, bearing a long and multi-colored beard, a mustache with the remnants of some meal still crusted on it, puffy cheeks, a round nose showing lots of broken capillaries, and small eyes reddened by too much sun or drink. He was hatless, and Leah noticed that he was balding. She didn't know how much longer she could stand his odors.

He grabbed her ponytail in one of his thick hands and, while still gripping her tightly, pulled her face back so she could look into her eyes.

"So, lady, who told you you could fish here?" he finally said.

She felt a surge of relief. He was angry with her for fishing, for god's sake. That meant he wasn't interested in raping her. Or at least she hoped that was the case.

"If you let me go, we can talk," she replied, struggling now to free herself from his grip.

"No, no. Not yet," he said, squeezing her tighter and entangling her hair more securely in his fingers. "First, you tell me what god-damned right you think you have to take my fish."

"Your fish?" Leah hadn't imagined that these were someone's private streams. She thought she might be able to pull off a joke. "Gee, I don't know why you're worrying about me. I sure haven't caught anything. Don't think I ever will, either!"

He took her seriously. "That don't matter. Let me see your creel."

Leah pointed to the creel. He bent down to kick it with his foot, still gripping her tightly. When he was satisfied that it was flat enough to be empty, he turned his attention back to her. She sensed his grip loosening and tried to move away. Instead, he increased the pressure on her taut ponytail.

"Lady. I'm telling you. Don't try to run away. You have some serious accounting here. You've sinned, you know. You came on my land."

He kicked the creel high into the air. It landed somewhere near the banks of the creek.

"I don't know what you mean. Look. Please let me go. I promise I won't try to run away. I promise. I'll listen. Please."

Leah hated the whine in her voice, but now she realized more than ever the peril she was in. He must be mad or alcohol-impaired. No one owned these lands. They were part of the Bureau of Land Management. She had every right to fish here; she had checked this out when she got her license and the regs. She would just have to calm him down somehow.

"Shut up, you little bitch. I do the talking here."

Now he put one of his hands over her mouth. Leah could taste some greasy substance. She bit him.

He yelped in pain and flung her down to the ground. Leah noted that it was growing dark, and she hoped she might evade him in the night, but as she looked up at the man, she noted that he was bent over but at the same time drawing from his jacket something like a gun. She didn't stir, keeping her face to the ground.

"Now you've done it," he raged. "I asked you before. Who do you think you are? Coming up here to the woods, to my river, with your fancy clothes, your L. L. Bean gear, your perfect little flies, your lipstick. You don't deserve to be in this spot. It belongs to me."

Oddly, his use of "L.L. Bean" reassured her. He couldn't be entirely a hermit if he was familiar with brand names. She decided to try to appeal to the intelligence which must be buried somewhere in that massive body.

"OK. OK. Only, please. If you let me go, I promise I won't come back here. I'll stay far away from your spot."

She turned toward him. She could barely make him out in the fading light. She arose, surprised he let her. But as soon as she felt relief at that, he reached out for her, grabbing her arm and pulling her to within a few inches of his face.

She tried to appeal again. "Absolutely. I will. I'll stay away." She meant it.

"Yeah." He pulled her closer.

She could smell the liquor. Her stomach crunched.

"You and your friend, that tall guy," he continued, "I've been watching you and him. You people just sashay in here as though you owned everything you touch. I can smell it: money, education, leisure time. You just come in and take over our fish. You just play with them. You get all gushy about the art of fishing, about how it gives you peace, like

138

going to a shrink. You moon over the color of the fish, the way their scales shine in the sun. You think they're something to be admired and put back, like some kind of painting in a museum. Well, they ain't that."

Leah tried to see his eyes clearer, sensing a glimmer of intelligence behind the ranting. She remained as still as she could.

Now his voice got louder, and the words tumbled together at a faster pace:

"As it is, the fish and game people ruin it for the rest of us, farming them and then stocking the streams. The ones you catch don't even have any flavor anymore 'cause they haven't had to fight for survival the way they used to. It's all because of you tourists coming into these parts and throwing your money around and wanting there to be plenty of fish, so you can spout poetry about what a mind-expanding experience it is to go fly fishing, how you all become one with the universe and all that crap. Wearing waders that haven't hardly been used, getting most of the rivers up here named as conservation waters, so we have to catch and release, can't rely on good fresh fish for dinner anymore. I hate you city people. I been watching you. I seen your car near here with those California license plates. Who the hell do you think you are?"

Leah noted that in one especially vehement part of his harangue, he loosened his grip on her. During his last tirade, he gestured wildly, and she slipped from his grasp. She picked up a small boulder and threw it at him. To her amazement, the rock found its mark, and he fell to the ground. She took the opportunity to turn and run, leaving her father's fishing rod and tackle box where they rested. She knew she had to escape, find cover somewhere, and wait until it was truly pitch-black to make her way home.

She ran faster than she ever had in her life, even though she didn't hear anyone behind her yet, tripping on loose shale at the base of the hills around her. She managed to stumble along until she saw a narrow trail. The problem was that she had to keep going up, toward more wilderness, instead of being able to follow it back down to familiar ground. He was that direction, and she had to avoid him at all costs. She continued deeper into the now thicker aspens and pines, the trail having more switchbacks and turns as it got progressively steeper.

Her way was often blocked by fallen logs or branches, and she could taste the salt of fear on her tongue, yet she stumbled on. Still she heard nothing behind her. Now she found herself in a deep stand of trees, conifers untouched by logging or thinning. She fell against one whose thick trunk must have been felled by lightning. It blocked her way and, in the increasing dark and her exhaustion, seemed almost insurmountable

Nonetheless, Leah found a branch and, placing one foot on it, hoisted herself over to the other side, the ragged bark ripping into one of her exposed elbows. She found shelter under the overhang of one of its largest branches and tucked herself under its thick needles. She glanced at her high-tech waterproof watch (Old Mountain Man was right in one sense; she did carry some of the latest gear) and noted that it was almost 10:00 p.m. She would wait another hour and, if she didn't hear him, try to find her way back down to the cabin.

Everything she would need to help her was left in the tackle box or in her car, parked on the roadway downstream. She felt in her pockets and noted that she didn't have a flashlight or any matches. She was still warm: at least she had the jacket she had put on just before she was grabbed by the monster.

The cell phone she had used to make her infrequent calls to Ned or her mother lay back on the kitchen table. Even her sharp knife was in the tackle box. All she had was her resolve. If he didn't show up, she was confident she could get to her house. She would avoid going near the car; obviously, he would assume she would try to get back there.

Maybe, though, he was through with her, just wanted to let off steam. Had he actually had a weapon? Had he posed any real danger? Even as she pondered this possibility, the reminder of his strength cancelled any thoughts that he was just spouting off. He had meant to hurt her.

Leah looked again at her watch. It was 10:10. She still hadn't heard anything. Maybe she could just go quietly now. No, she must stick to her previous plan. By 11:00, it would be ink dark, and that would help in case she sensed him near. She had to be patient.

She moved a bit in the close space, allowed her now-cramped legs to stretch. She let them creep out a bit beyond the shelter of the branches, and as she rearranged her feet, she found she could just sit up enough to rest back against a clump of foliage.

Several more minutes passed, and Leah felt the ground beneath her hand turn colder. She grabbed a few pine needles and lifted them to her nose. They held the redolent green of life. Robert Jordan, in *For Whom the Bell Tolls*, had felt the same sensory pleasure as he lay ready for death on that Spanish hillside. She had always loved that passage, what it said about the beauties available to us as we live. The scent of pine, the good earth. She felt around the tree for a small stone and then put it in her pocket, a memento of this nightmare.

She shivered now, brought her legs in to curl up on her side in a fetal position. Still, she heard no footsteps.

What irony, if her attacker should find her, wreak his warped vengeance and anger (now justified with the headache she'd given him) upon her, and kill her. She had chosen not to die, as least not yet. By coming here to Idaho and reevaluating her life and the treatments available, she sensed deep down inside her that she had opted for another chance. She knew she would keep trying as long as she could see the faces of her sons, as long as she could communicate her love to them, as long as she could have Ned by her side. *Ned.* It was Ned she thought of, not Adam. Her Ned, the man who had seen her through all the bad, who would do everything he could to help her again if she opted for more Interferon. Well, like the cell phone, she wryly noted, he wasn't here now. She'd have to do this alone; she'd have to survive this new challenge. In the long run, she knew she would always have to survive and, if necessary, die alone. That didn't mean she couldn't give and receive comfort along the way. She needed to tell Ned that she loved him. She needed to hold her sons again.

"It takes life to love life," Lucinda Matlock had said in one of her favorite poems. Well, she'd take life in any way she could.

Just then, she heard a sound in the brush nearby. Was it a footfall? She stilled herself, not even wanting her pounding heart to sound in the air. She felt herself shrivel up, as if by being smaller he couldn't find her, like she and Jeannette used to feel when they played hide-and-go-seek. Shhh! Quiet as a church mouse. Her back itched.

She waited for further sound, heard something rustling nearby, and stopped breathing for a few seconds. Then, to her shock, she heard a rush of leaves only a few feet from her, felt the creature hurtle closer to her and, in fact, leap over her hiding place. Some small animal, she knew, with a wash of relief. Still, she didn't move, just in case her perceptions were wishful thinking.

She looked at her watch, glowing in the dark with the time 10:50. It was dark enough now, she thought, dark enough to stir from this place and head back down the hill, with no compass or flashlight, but the side of slopes downward to signal the right direction. She crawled out of her spot and, leaning against the scratchy surface of the tree, righted herself. She ached with fatigue and fear, but made her way back over the huge trunk and slowly, carefully, felt her way down the hillside and through the thickets until, at about midnight, she spotted the hood of her car gleaming in a patch of moonlight.

She stopped, awaiting a sense of the presence of the large man nearby, but heard nothing. Now it struck her that she may have really hurt him. What if he were lying near the fishing spot bleeding to death? What if she were responsible for that? Still, she couldn't trust getting into her car. He might even be in there. Again, like a child, she was caught in an unreasonable fear based on ghost stories or urban legends. What if he were lying under the car with a knife ready to slash her ankles when she tried to get in? Or what if he was crouching in the back seat, ready to pull his gun on her when she put the key in the ignition? Too many movies, too much imagination, too many Freddy Kruegers.

Anyway, where were her keys? In the tackle box! So it was moot. She would have to stick to plan A and get down the road somehow without her car. She slipped up the trail, running along the road, and stepped above it a few feet so she could not be seen. She made her way, step by laborious step, a few hundred yards along the path, grabbing the thin trunks of saplings for support, until she could no longer see the car on the road behind her.

Her mother's AA philosophy came to mind. One day at a time. One step at a time. "Put one foot in front of the other and keep going. That's the only way to get through this," she'd recalled her mother advising her during the Interferon treatments. With the Interferon, it was often one minute at a time. Wait for the pain to disappear, bend into it for a few seconds, know that it will pass, then get on to the next minute. She'd done that then, and she'd do it now. Still, she had a sense at the back of her neck that she wasn't alone. Just keep moving, keep going. One quiet step at a time.

At 3:00 a.m., she saw the slant of roof of the cabin and ran now toward it, toward the sanctuary it represented. She unearthed the hidden extra key from beneath the pot of marigolds and opened the door to the warmth within. Without even turning on a light in the space she knew so well, she found her cell phone and dialed 911.

Chapter Twenty-One

L eah sat with her feet tucked up under her on the old sofa, the loose afghan around her and a cup of tea warming her hands. Adam and a uniformed sheriff sat in front of her on chairs they had pulled up. She was trying now to tell the exact location of the encounter with the mountain man. She'd been through most of the story but was striving to be clear so the men who had been dispatched to find him could not waste any more time than necessary. Now she heard the first officer, seated at her kitchen table, talking on the phone to them.

"Yep. You found the car? Well, you're not far from about where she said she was fishing. He's probably upstream a few hundred yards. OK. Let us know if you find him."

Leah turned now to Adam, who had surprised her with his appearance. The sheriffs had responded within just a few minutes of her call, and she had felt overwhelming relief when she heard their car pulling in the driveway. But she had been shocked to see the familiar figure of Adam behind them as they came in the door. Now that she knew they had sent a search party, she turned to him.

"Oh, and thanks for the tea." She paused, taking a sip. She looked into his deep-set eyes. "Come to think of it, though, what were you doing with these officers?" She realized now that she was shaking.

"I came by about 10:00 tonight to check up on you. When I realized your car was gone, I waited for a while, and when you didn't come here, I got worried. I called Betty, thinking maybe you'd decided to go home to California. Woke her up, but she said she hadn't heard anything about it, figured you would let her know when you were leaving, so she could close up the place, and so on.

"Anyway, I thought maybe you'd gone fishing, but it worried me that you were this late, alone and stuff. So I drove up to the river and saw your car. I called out a few times, even tried to get to the river, but then decided that I'd better call the sheriff."

Adam looked at Leah, searching for a reaction.

"When I went to them, they said that there really wasn't any reason to search at this time, so I left them my number and asked them to call me if they heard anything. I drove back up to your car and shouted out for you again a few times, then figured that it would be best just to wait at the sheriff's station until they decided to do something about it. So that's why I was with them when you finally called. I followed them over here."

So the orangutan called, Leah thought. She chuckled at her own grisly joke and saw Adam studying her. She stared back. He was an awfully attractive big ape. It was unfair. And of course, he hadn't raped her. Not by a long shot. It had certainly been consensual. Odd thing was, though, she felt a distance from him, wasn't sure she wanted him around, and felt a pang of remorse at the thought.

She wanted to be able to call Ned, to tell him all about the scare. She wanted privacy.

The sheriff who had been on the phone now came toward her, his Smokey the Bear hat in hand. She recalled his name. Officer Jackson. Pete. Peter Jackson. He was very thin

146

and youthful looking, with a pronounced Adam's apple and a thatch of blonde hair marked with a ring where the hat's brim had rested. He didn't look much older than Tim. Before she knew it, she thought, *Not so far from now, Tim would be this age.* Hot tears spring to her eyes.

"Excuse me, ma'am? Mrs. Brown?" He waited for her to place her full attention with him.

"Our men are up where your car is and have started by now to go upstream to the scene of the attack. I've given them all the information you shared with us. I guess we'll just have to wait." Leah motioned him to sit down, but he shook his head and continued, still standing at attention.

"You know, this is the first time we've had something like this happen up here. We've had reports of a cranky old guy up there. Nickname's Moose. But we don't think he's ever been real threatening before. Hard to imagine he'd get so crazy like that."

He paused and, when he got no response, said, "Are you OK? I mean, will you be OK? One of us will stay here with you until we apprehend the suspect."

Adam arose now and directed his comments to the officer.

"Thank you, Pete, but that won't be necessary. I'll stay here with Mrs. Brown."

Leah glanced at the young officer, gauging his reaction.

"Well, sir," he said, "I appreciate your help, but in a case like this, we really have to stay here."

To Leah's surprise, Adam didn't let this go. "Oh really? How many cases like this have you worked?"

Leah didn't like that tone, found herself interrupting. "That's fine, Adam. I'd really like one of the officers to stay. I've been the source of enough sleeplessness to you tonight already."

She was surprised by the tone of dismissal in her voice. She realized it was the wrong person deciding issues for her. Ned, her usual protector, should be standing here instead of Adam.

"I really think you should go home and grab some sleep," she said. "I promise. I'll call you when we have any news."

Adam's face looked abashed, as though he'd just received a scolding from his mother. Those fine strong features softened more than she'd ever noticed before. But he grabbed his hat from the couch's armrest, tipped it to her, and turned around. At the door, he looked back at Leah.

"OK. If that's the way you want it. If you're sure."

When he saw by the look in her eyes that she was, he opened the door and left. She heard his truck start up and then drive away. She turned her attention to the two officers before her.

"You both don't have to stay. I'm fine, really." Leah was telling herself that she would stop shaking soon, that now she was just upset by sending Adam away. Maybe without his alien (*alien?*) presence she would feel better. Ned. She had to talk to Ned.

"Mrs. Brown?" Pete was saying. "I'm going to stay here in the living room while Officer Briggs joins the search. He'll come back for me later. I hope that's OK. We'll help you to your room if you feel like resting."

Balm in Gilead again. Leah felt a rush of release and relief, let herself be helped up and taken to the retreat of her bedroom.

Still shaking, she nonetheless thanked Officer Briggs and asked Pete to bring her the cell phone. She closed the door, secure with the benign presence of the young officer, heard the other officer close the front door, start up the car and drive away, and then she sat on the bed. The corduroy of the duvet was warm and comforting under her palms. Finally, she stilled her shaking hand to call home and let it ring long enough in the early California morning to awaken Ned.

His voice, so familiar and true, answered.

Leah spilled out the events of the night, with Ned's reassuring comments sustaining her account.

Finally Ned said, "Do you want me to come up?"

Leah went with her first instinct. "No. I'm OK. There's an officer staying here. They'll get the guy, I'm sure, and then I'll get my car. I'm sure everything will be fine."

Ned's voice now carried a stronger tone of authority. "There's another option, you know. You could come home as soon as you get the car. Please, Leah, consider just wrapping things up. I want you here where you are safe."

To her surprise, Leah didn't resent his strength. She knew he spoke from love, not the need to control. "I'm thinking about it. I have something to finish up here, and then I'll be home. I promise."

"OK. But if you need me up there, please call. I'll be there within hours. Oh, and I wanted to tell you something. Think now might be a good time. I've been thinking about us. About our problems."

Leah felt a roll in her abdomen. "Yes?"

"Well, I think we, or at least I, need help. I mean, to deal with all this, the illness, our issues, the marriage. I made an appointment with a counselor. I'm going to go see her next week. If you want to come, we can both do it, but I don't care. I'll go by myself if it might help."

Leah couldn't respond, let the words sink in as Ned went on.

"Anyway, I love you, I want our marriage to be strong, and I'm willing to do anything to make it so. Is that OK?"

"Of course, Ned." Leah found her voice. "We'll talk about this when I get home. In the meantime, all I can say is thank you."

Mr. Fixit, her dear, a man who would take the initiative in something like this.

"Thanks. I think I can sleep now, so I'll hang up. Be careful and safe. Love you."

As Leah said these words, she felt them truly for the first time in years. She *did* love Ned. Whether or not that was enough was something else.

"Well, then, the same to you." Ned's voice was gone.

Leah went to the bathroom and shed her clothes, leaving them on the floor. She stepped into the small stall shower and turned on the water with as much force and heat she could stand. She let the water beat upon her tired back. Then she toweled off, put on her nightgown and the robe hanging from a hook, and padded to the bedroom door. She opened it slightly, sticking her head through the narrow space.

"Officer Jackson?" Leah saw that the young sheriff was sitting on a chair facing the front door, his rifle on his lap. He turned to look at her. "I think I'm ready to get some sleep. I just want to thank you for being here. I feel safe."

Peter Jackson smiled shyly. "Just doing my job, ma'am. Don't worry about anything. We'll get old Moose. Oh, and we'll get your car after we bring him in. As I said, don't worry about anything."

"Well, thanks again. Good night."

Leah closed the door, went to the dresser and pulled out her nightgown, took off her robe and put on the gown, then snuggled under the comforter, and fell instantly asleep.

Chapter Twenty-Two

March 10, 1864

Our family now numbers three. Two days ago, I bore a daughter, whom we named Helen Ingrid in honor of the two women who stay in my thoughts at all times. She is precious and healthy, and I feel blessed. I am being allowed this relatively long period of rest because of Bethanne's generous spirit. She is the one who must be tired, as she acted as midwife during the twenty-six hours from the onset of my first labor pains until Helen's arrival in this world. Thaddeus waited until the baby was clean and then weighed her in a scale he keeps in his office. She weighs seven pounds and has been already an eager and hungry baby. My milk has come in and I feel quite content. She sleeps next to me while I write this. Thaddeus has almost completed a lovely little cradle he made for me in secret at night while I fell asleep exhausted these past few weeks.

I am hoping to resume my work with Bethanne in a few days. She has some temporary help from one of the women who is with a party testing the waters of mining in this area, but I fear that will not be for very long, and I have an obligation to contribute my share of the chores.

Helen is awakening now, ready to have some nourishment. My entries in this journal may be considerably shorter with the added but wonderful demands of my life, her life.

*****

(I am so tired that I feel as though I never want to leave this bed. I remember my mother's friends discussing childbirth and sharing their fearsome stories, and now I understand their meaning. I am just happy that I have Helen, but the labor was certainly that! I am also lucky that Bethanne was so efficient and knew what to do, for I fear that without her at my side, I wouldn't have survived. With God's mercy, I am beginning to forget the pains of two days ago, but I really don't know if I would choose to have another child—that is, if it were my choice. It is up to the men of the world, in every sense. I can't say no to my husband. Right this minute, I do not feel like ever again giving him my body.

I was helping Bethanne fold some laundry in the early morning when the first pain struck, and it was so severe that I had to sit down. I did not have another for several minutes, but Bethanne urged me to go upstairs to my room and prepare for the birth. I did as she said, and she kept checking in with me every few minutes. I must say that being alone was the hardest thing to bear during the day of my labor. When I would hear her footsteps ascending toward our bedroom, I would have the only moments of peace I experienced during the long ordeal.

Thaddeus had to stay at the claims office and could not help. Poor man. When he finally did get away to visit me at our bedside, he did not seem to know what to do. He fled as soon as he could, using the business as an excuse, I suspect. I know this is woman's business, really, and I don't blame him. He was there for one of my contractions, and I saw him blanch, and while he held my hand, he could not look me in the eyes. He left as soon as he could let my hand go and did not return until late in the night. By that time, I was having pains every couple of minutes, and he could only step outside the room and pace. I didn't see him after his last visit until the baby was born at 10:00 a.m. the next day. I don't believe men want to face what happens as a result of their desires.

At one time, I screamed out for him. I cannot tell anyone who has not been through this the extent of the pain. I felt as though my insides were being pulled out. Even as I am thinking this, I feel that I am being a crybaby; after all, women have always had this pain. Now I know why my mother calls our natural cycle the curse. Perhaps it *was* Eve's punishment, borne by women ever since her sin. I know it is the necessary process by which new life is created, and I understand that anything so magical requires a severe price, but still, at the time, I wondered why it had to be so awfully excruciating. I know in my heart that Thaddeus couldn't have done anything to relieve the agony, and I understand his feelings of helplessness. Again, I tell myself, it *is* woman's business. But I yearned to have him with me.

After the birth, when he did come in to see Helen, he was most sweet and tender. He was bearing a small cradle he promised is nearly done (it needs a coat of varnish, he says.) He looked quite disheveled and timid. For such a strong man, he seemed daunted by the whole event. He couldn't bear to hold Helen, but he did smile at her most tenderly and called out her name softly. He also leaned over me and gave me a brief kiss "in honor of your efforts," he said. He then fled to the sanctuary of his toilette and a change of clothes and then the claims office.

Later Bethanne told me that he had spent the whole night in the hallway by my door. While he couldn't bear to come in, he wanted to be near, she felt.

Dear Bethanne. After she had finished serving dinner and then cleaning up, she was able to sit with me during the rest of the long night. We do have a doctor in town, a rather disreputable character who ministers to the accidents of the miners and fills out death certificates, but he was drunk when Bethanne went to see him to ask him to help. He gave her some instructions and told her to send for him if things went wrong. Both of us agreed that we did not want to use him if we didn't have to. She actually did the work of delivering the baby and cutting her cord. If I hadn't had Bethanne, I shudder to think of the loneliness I would have felt. As it was, I craved the company of good women, especially wishing that Ingrid could be here. I miss the comfort of women's warmth.

When Thaddeus and I decide what our next path is, I'm going to write Ingrid and see if she wishes to join us. Thaddeus has agreed. Perhaps he feels that he will not have to put up with such a complaining wife if I have female company.)

*****

August 8, 1998

The girl was running, her ponytail bobbing in the wind off the ocean. She was crying now, as a shape gained on her. The shape wore a sailor hat, and as it came closer, the girl could begin to make out the features. She dared not look behind, just knew she must run faster through the crowds of people on the pier. Her white ballerina shoes were not adequate for the job of running, but she tried and finally dodged into a building whose sides were painted with grotesque figures. She closed the door and entered a corridor leading to a large room. When she heard the door open and close behind her, she dashed into the room, which was filed with mirrors distorting her image. She tried to find her way out, but as she did, she noticed that each mirror reflected a different view of her. In one, her body was elongated, her neck so thin it looked as though it couldn't support her neck. In the next, she was squashed down to the flattened image of a dwarf, and in the next, her body parts were separated. She stared into that one, temporarily mesmerized by the puzzle. How had they done it? As she gazed into the framed mirror, she heard the door behind her open, saw the monster shape of a disembodied sailor beret floating behind her image.

"Mrs. Brown? Are you OK? Mrs. Brown?"

There was a light tapping on her door. Leah sat up in bed, awakening from her nightmare. *Sailors. Moose.* Figures chasing her, natural nightmares after her ordeal of the night before. She realized that the voice calling her was Pete Jackson's. The young sheriff. Out of her fog, she answered.

"It's OK, Pete. I'm OK. Thanks. Just a nightmare."

She looked over at the alarm clock and noted that it was 8:00, threw back the comforter and stepped into her slippers. Then she wrapped herself in her robe, ran her fingers through her hair, and went into the main room of the cabin. Young Officer Jackson was standing near the bedroom door.

"Morning," Leah said to him as she traversed the small room to the end of the kitchen. "How about some coffee?" She poured water into the teapot and set it on the flame.

"Sure. Thanks," the young man said, still standing in the same place, as if on guard. "I heard you saying something in there. Sorry if I woke you."

As Leah ground the beans and put them in the filter, the water started boiling. She loved a gas stove. As they continued to exchange pleasantries, Leah finished making two cups of rich coffee and motioned to Officer Jackson to sit with her at the table.

As they sat and sipped the steaming brew, Leah asked the question that had been on her mind since she first remembered this morning the presence of a sheriff's deputy in her house.

"So what's up? What's the news? Did you find Moose or whoever that character was?"

Pete smiled. "As a matter of fact, yes. At dawn this morning, I got a call from the office. They had the suspect in custody. Guess they found him around 6:00 a.m., right where you said you left him."

"So was he OK? I mean, I think I may have hurt him with that rock."

"He was asleep when they found him. Dead to the world, so to speak." He smiled again, and Leah noticed that he had brilliant white teeth. Modern dentistry's bleaching miracles, even up here in the boonies. He continued, "He didn't remember much of what had happened. Had a large bump on his forehead. I guess you did stun him."

"So why do you think he was still out when you found him?" Leah asked.

"I'm not sure, but they gave him a Breathalyzer and he had so much alcohol in his blood that we figure he was ready to pass out when you hit him with your rock, and he must have just zonked. Oh, and by the way, we didn't find a gun anywhere. There was a thick wooden spoon nearby, but that was it."

Leah took in this information as she sipped the comforting hot coffee. Her attacker hadn't been armed. The monster was so drunk that he probably couldn't have hurt her much, except that he was huge and frightening in his strength. She thought of her dream, the disembodied specter chasing her through the fun house. Was that an image of Moose, of her fears, of the subconscious bogeyman left over from childhood? She decided to table her feelings about this until later when she was alone.

"Would you like some toast or something?" she said now to the officer fingering the stubble of blonde beard.

"No, thanks. If you think you're OK, I'll go now. I've got to check in at the office and sign out, shower, and stuff." He looked into Leah's eyes. "Now tell me. Are you sure you're OK?"

"I'm fine."

"Good. We'll need you to come down later. Your car's out front. Officer Jenkins brought it down."

Leah noticed the keys on the coffee table, couldn't imagine that she had slept through the comings and goings of the night.

Leah rose, as did Pete, then saw him to the door, reassuring him and thanking him for his help. When she returned to the kitchen sink and made herself another cup of coffee, she knew what her next step would be. She needed to talk to her mother.

Chapter Twenty-Three

April 14, 1864

his evening when Thaddeus came home from the claims office, he had a formal document in one hand. He took baby Helen in his arms as he passed it to me to read. It seems that we are the proud recipients of a homesteading parcel of land a few miles away from here. I haven't seen the property, but Thaddeus has assured me that it is in a large green meadow along the river, a place of trees and grasses and less perilous banks and gullies. The other day, he rode out to claim it when he heard from the government that they had opened up this part of Idaho Territory for homesteading.

I actually saw Thaddeus smile as he has not since we first were married. He says he feels that he has finally seen the light at the end of the tunnel. Only now do I realize how burdened he has been in the past several months, missing the chance to continue on to Oregon territory with his pregnant wife complaining about the change of plans! And I am sure that he has not enjoyed the work here. Thaddeus is a man who is destined to work the earth.

I arose and went to Thaddeus, putting my arm around him as I also cradled the baby with the other. I do believe that our little family will now be set aright and that we will be much happier as we settle into our new place.

Thaddeus has asked the Murphys if we can stay on here until he gets some form of shelter for us, and they have agreed. He has thought of many things, and I realize that he has been planning this for a long time. He has even hired a helper for the summer, one of the young men who have been so disillusioned by the reality of not striking it rich. Thaddeus is determined to build at least one room with a big fireplace so that by next winter, we can be warm and protected. He promises to chink the logs carefully so we will not experience the drafts we have here in this hotel.

I trust him completely in this effort, especially as I see how the prospect of working with his hands causes his eyes to light up. He has saved enough money from his work with the claims office that we can put in sufficient provisions for that first winter.

I am in awe of his confidence and yet glad that I can remain here for a few more months while Thaddeus constructs our home. He will camp there during the upcoming summer months, and I shall probably not see very much of him, but at least I will have Bethanne and Helen for companionship.

Much of the snow is finally off the ground, and I am able to see the tiny heads of crocus in the small bed of flowers outside the hotel door. I imagine an emotion shared by women throughout all of time, the joy at the prospect of spring and the warm sun on our arms.

Thaddeus leaves in two weeks, as soon as he has trained a replacement for the office. I can almost feel the rush of energy he experiences as he draws his simple plans for the home and reads up on farming methods in the agricultural journals he had intended to use in Oregon. Now they may prove our salvation as we attempt a living from the soil of Idaho.

*****

May 24, 1864

Yesterday I left the security of Miner's Rest for the first time in all the months since we first arrived there. Helen was strapped in a papoose-like contraption wrapped around my back and shoulders so that she rested her head above my bosom as we mounted the horses. Once we set off on our journey of some eleven miles northwest, she fell fast asleep and did not utter a whimper the whole time. Her breathing matched the rhythm of the hooves beneath us. We made our way many miles over trails, though still perilous, that had been widened by traffic, but I noticed that the landscape started to gentle as we neared our destination. The slopes became less steep, and I could see the mountains beginning to recede from my immediate vision into a part of the scene farther and farther away from us. As we neared the site of our new home, I felt my heart beating fiercely. What if it wasn't as beautiful as I had imagined? What if the valley echoed the dismal sage desert of the trip we made on the Oregon Trail? I was not sure I could bear yet another disappointment.

But as we came to the top of a bend in the hills, Thaddeus asked me to stop behind him and then came over to my horse, helping me dismount with our sleeping baby. He then told me to trust him by closing my eyes until he told me to look. Of course I did so, my mind prepared for palliative and insincere words should the sight prove dismal. He led me slowly up a small rise of the path and then asked me to open my eyes. As I write this, I am afraid that my tears may wet the pages, for the view before me was entirely unlike what I had expected.

Before us lay the loveliest small valley awash with the fierce blue of some kind of wildflower! Occasional patches of a vivid yellow also dotted the hills that fringed the rolling meadows, craggy mountains in the distance. I could not breathe for happiness and would not let Thaddeus release me from his grip for several minutes. Off to the right, perhaps five hundred yards from us on a small hillock, was a cleared patch of ground, a pile of logs and the beginnings of a chimney made from some kind of grayish rock.

I turned to Thaddeus and, as I leant closer to his rough wool jacket, spoke the words I knew he wanted to hear.

"Oh my. It's beautiful! I love it here. Thank you."

We remounted our horses and rode to the site of the house. As I stood on the space where we would place our small table and chairs and eventually share family meals together, I asked Thaddeus to share a prayer with me. We bent our knees to the rough ground and knelt there.

"Lord," I prayed, "thank you for this abundance and bless our home."

The nice thing was that I meant it.

I can envision sitting in my warm home and then going out to enjoy the trees that shadow the rear of the house. To the front is a rather level plateau, but I can see a creek running nearby to the east.

Our conversation now is filled with the plans we have made these past few months. Thaddeus has already started the planting of root vegetables like potatoes and beets. I believe Billy, his helper, may even choose to join us this winter. He is inquiring about homesteading possibilities nearby.

I have been deluging poor Bethanne with all the details since our return today. Thaddeus has already left to resume his work on the house, and I will probably not see him until the middle of June. He took the extra horse and a mule loaded with provisions so that he and Billy can work uninterrupted.

*****

(As happy as I am with the beauty and hope embodied in our new land, I am fearful that Thaddeus and I are still not as close as I would wish. He could hardly bear to stay with me last night until he could get the gear ready and depart for the land. I understand that he is thinking about our family and all that this means, but deep in my heart, I wonder if the real, the physical me, is apart from his true feelings. I fear he sees me as a wife and mother, not as Linnea Milton, the still young woman he once wanted to hold.

Last night, as we both put the blankets over our night-clothes, shivering in the still-cold Idaho night, I put my arms around his back. He did not respond. At first I thought perhaps he was asleep, tired from the trip home to Miner's Rest and then the readying of supplies, but I arose on my elbow just enough to catch a glance of his left cheek. His eyes were not closed, and they seemed fixed on something very far away. I gently nudged him and whispered, "Thaddeus? Thaddeus, my love?"

Still, he didn't respond, so I began stroking his back. To my surprise, he reached back and grabbed my hand and then clasped it along his belly under his strong arms and fingers so that I could not rub him further. On the one hand, I can view this as a means to get me closer to him, but at the same time, I felt rebuffed. I had hoped that he would express some passion for me, especially as we have rarely been together in a married sense since Helen's birth. Actually, he did not even say good night. A few minutes afterward, he began to snore, and I knew that my desires had been dismissed.

I wonder if all men are alike in their concentration on the task at hand or on the work they do, whatever it may be. We women, I believe, spend more time dealing with matters of the heart. I may have to accept that this is the essential difference between us as man and wife, but I do not have to like it. I feel this urge to share my feelings and hopes with Thaddeus, while he just seems to want to get on with the realities of life, not frittering away a minute, as he might put it, on wasted emotions and energy. I ache for him tonight.)

*****

October 1864

I am writing this at the rough-hewn table Thaddeus created out of scraps from the logs which surround me in our new home. I know that someday we will have finer things, but for now, I am most grateful to be able to sit in this small room which I can call my own. Helen sleeps nearby in her cradle, which she will soon outgrow. Thaddeus has fashioned a small bed for her at the foot of ours. Our bed is just across from me, nestled against the chinked logs which are the same both outside and inside. I know they will serve us well even in the winter cold. We also have a rocking chair, which I will pull up close to the fireplace on winter evenings. So the bed, the chair, the table, and two benches are our only furnishings at the moment, but I am content.

We were surprised this summer at Miner's Rest by a visit from four of the soldiers stationed at Fort Boise. They brought us our remaining possessions. Thaddeus had planned to ride down there one day and arrange some transport, but the young men, possibly out of curiosity to see a true gold rush town, had convinced their senior officers to undertake the journey on their own.

When I saw the pile of boxes and trunks, I wept. They seemed like ghosts from some other life. I couldn't wait for Thaddeus and opened one small trunk that Ingrid had helped me pack. I remember clearly the conversation we had as we folded the items in our shared bedroom in Boston.

"Here," Ingrid had said, as she carefully draped tissue paper around her favorite satin dress, the one whose cornflower blue matched her eyes so well, "I want you to take this dress... the one you always so admired. I want to picture you in it, dancing with your new friends at parties in Oregon."

"Oh, Ingrid," I remember saying as tears rolled down my cheeks. "It's your best dress. I can't do that!"

I recall how firm she was when she made a space in the trunk for it. "Of course you can. It is easy for me to get another dress. I don't imagine you will have much time to sew for yourself for a very long while, and I insist."

As I unfolded it and saw that it had not been damaged by rain or water and was, indeed, the soft, silken fabric I remembered, I was overcome by two emotions, a longing for my sister and the rest of my family, and gratitude for having survived long enough to be able to enjoy her gift. I shall wear it sometime soon.

I also found the baby clothes that my mother had tucked in the trunk. One wee smock, in a pink calico, is slightly too large for Helen, but I dressed her in it anyway. Bethanne said I should have named her Rose, as the warm hues befit her sweet coloring. We enjoyed showing her off to several of the hotel guests before reluctantly taking the dress off and replacing it, with Ingrid's cornflower-blue gown, in the trunk.

I wonder if my life will ever be civilized enough to dare to wear such a treasure.

Shortly before I said my goodbyes to the hotel and left with Thaddeus for our home, Bethanne received a letter via the Pony Express, which gives me hope that I may soon hear from Ingrid. Thaddeus can occasionally make trips back to Miner's Rest by horseback, and so we will use the hotel as our post office. I pray that Ingrid has received the letters I have sent to her.

So here I sit, the quiet of the surrounding landscape so intense as almost to create a sound of its own. Somewhere, many acres *from here, Thaddeus is working with Billy to plant the bulbs for spring growth, and except for my sleeping baby, I am alone. I am very alone. Billy did construct a small extra room off the back of our one-room so that he will not disturb our privacy, but he joins us for meals. I am actually glad of the company. Thaddeus and I talk, but he is usually so exhausted when he returns for dinner that our exchanges are brief. Often he falls asleep on our bed with his clothes still on.*

There is a definite chill in the air, nights are cold. We have provisions enough for the winter, and Thaddeus says he will go hunting in a couple of days to get us some venison.

Although I am wanting female company, I have plenty to do. I am repairing the clothes damaged by hard work and the trip on the Oregon Trail, making a patchwork quilt for Helen's new bed, and spending much of my time thinking about the reality that I am once again with child. I expect the baby to arrive toward the end of April. I can use the time this winter to be with my sweet Helen and learn some of the crafts that may prove useful to my role as a homesteader.

If the child is a boy, Thaddeus will want to name him after his departed brother Jacob. If the baby is a girl, I plan on calling her Bethanne.

Chapter Twenty-Four

Leah heard her mother's phone ring and the answering machine begin: "You have reached Barbara Ames. I am unable to come to the phone but will be glad to return your call. Please leave a message after the beep."

Like mother, like daughter, Leah thought. *She's giving out more information than necessary as a woman living alone.* At the end of the message, her mother picked up.

"Hello? Hello?"

"Mom, it's Leah."

"Oh, hi, darling. Sorry you had to sit through the message. I was in the garden."

Leah could picture her mother in worn jeans and the old floppy hat she wore for her outdoor chores. The small fenced yard in the back of the cottage in San Rafael must be bursting with blooms now. After all, it was a mature garden lovingly tended for years by her mother, whose green thumb Leah had not inherited. It provided a place of quiet reflection for anyone who was lucky enough to rest on the small wrought-iron bench in the northeast corner of the bricked patio. Leah could almost smell the orange blossoms and see the sweet peas climbing the trellis. Suddenly, she longed to be there, to hold her mother even for a few moments.

She was surprised at the crack in her voice, had trouble controlling it.

"Mom? Listen. First, I want you to change your message. You don't have to mention your name."

"Why, dear?" her mother replied.

"Just take my word for it. You're giving the signal that you are a woman alone. I don't want some stranger hearing that and finding out where you live."

"Oh, darling. You're being *too* dramatic. I'm just an old woman. Of course, it makes you feel better, I'll change it. But that's not why you called. What's going on?"

"Oh, nothing much." Leah caught herself smiling ruefully to herself. *Sure. Not much. Just the grand decision about Interferon, just being attacked by a monster, just an almost-shattered marriage. Not much.* She continued.

"I did have a run-in with a strange person, kind of a mountain man. Left me feeling a bit shaky, but I'm fine and he's in jail. In case you talk to Ned, I just thought you should know." Leah filled her mother in on the details.

Finally, once her mother seemed reassured that Leah was safe, she got to the point of her call.

"Mom? I wanted to ask you a favor. If I should start on this new regimen of Interferon, could you arrange to clear your schedule a bit and actually stay in our house for a few days, sort of be there for the boys?"

"Of course," her mother replied. "You know I will. I'll check at work and see how the calendar is for the next few weeks. When were you thinking of beginning?"

Leah knew her mother was aware of the devastation the last series of injections had wreaked on their household. She was reluctant to enlist her mother again, but felt that her decision would have to be based on the knowledge that there was extra support for Tim and Jeff, someone to be there when they came home from school.

"I'm not absolutely sure I'm even going to do this, just lining up my duckies, you know. But if I do, I'd guess it will be in three or four weeks, just about the time the boys start school. I'm considering the options."

The phone was quiet for a while, until Leah heard her mother's voice again, this time shaky and distant.

"Options? Is there something new I don't know about?"

Barbara Ames, whose voice reflected her concern, sat at the weathered oak table in her kitchen and twisted the spiral telephone cord around and then off her fingers. God, she hated this conversation!

"Nothing new. The dose would just be stronger, that's all. I'm not sure I want to put my family through this again."

"Well, dear," her mother said, now having to reach for a Kleenex as she choked out her words, "seems to me that the other option is unthinkable. You can't give up." Barbara knew this was simply advice from someone who feared her daughter's further decline.

"I know, Mom. But I just have to understand all of the consequences of my decision." A flash of memory of her kneeling on the shag carpet of her bathroom with Ned holding her as she vomited for the tenth time in four hours, hit her with a force. Ned, exhausted in his old sloppy T-shirt, with tears in his eyes at her pain. Not at his, but at hers. Ned, who had to present a major proposal for their most prestigious account the next morning at 10:00 a.m., perspiring as he held her in a too-warm room while she was wracked with chills icing through her body in waves. Ned, holding her, putting damp cool cloths on her forehead, not just a few times, but every single night she had an injection, losing sleep over her. Ned, getting up early enough to fix breakfast and lunch for the boys. Ned, sitting in the wing chair he'd pulled up to her bed after work, dozing off during the 6:00 evening news. Ned, who hadn't been able to finish *The Perfect Storm*, a book his sailing buddies had given him at the birthday dinner she'd missed last year because he had finally fallen asleep that afternoon after two sleepless nights.

"Mom?" she asked, reassured at the simple sound of that word. "Mom? Don't worry, I'm going to do the right thing. Listen, one other favor. Can you check something in Grandmother Emily's Bible?"

The thick leather-bound family Bible that Barbara had taken from her mother's home just before Emily Milton Danning's funeral lay now on the coffee table in her daughter's home. In the back was a place where there was a family history of sorts.

"Sure, dear. What do you need to know?"

"Well, I'd like to know if Grandmother listed the names of her grandfather's brothers and sisters. You know, Linnea's offspring. I remember seeing his name there and Grandmother's. But I wasn't that interested at the time about the others. Could you check and call me back on my cell phone here? I have to go into town about the incident last night, but I should be back by mid-afternoon."

"Of course. I'll call you later. Love you."

"Love you too, Mother."

*****

December 14, 1864

Our little home is now ready for the holidays. I had everything prepared, as my mother always did, by Lucia Day, and I am feeling quite proud that the pepperkakar and spritz cookies are done and stored near our potatoes in the cool shelves. I fashioned candles of my own, and tonight, Thaddeus will bring in a small tree from the nearby forest so that I can tie them to the branches in the holders I have made. For hours this morning, I strung cranberries to put on the tree. I think even Thaddeus is feeling festive. After all, we have done well so far this winter. We have been told that it is a relatively mild one, as there are only a few inches of snow. We are well stocked with firewood, and our food coffers are still quite full, so I am feeling optimistic.

I have finished gifts for my family: a flannel shirt for Thaddeus and a rag doll for Helen. Thaddeus has been working on a smaller version of her cradle to hold the doll. He spends nights whittling by the fire.

I am so happy that we did not leave behind on the trail the crate that contained our books. I am sustained daily by the words of the Bible and Shakespeare. I can't imagine what I would do without this escape into the world. I am reading The Tempest now and finding that if I can spend a few minutes a day on Prospero's island, I am able to more fully bear the isolation I feel here.

Billy went back into Miner's Rest a few weeks ago to earn some money toward things he will need when he begins to construct his home on the acres near us he now owns. I miss him a great deal; at the time, I often disparaged his offbeat sense of humor, but now I would crave his voice blended with ours at mealtimes. My secret hope is that he will bring home a bride with him in the spring, someone I can see occasionally and share more womanly subjects with.

One thing I wish I could speak with someone about is the way this pregnancy is so different from the first. I am truly very tired and nauseated most of the time. I know I have become thinner even though I should be getting ripe and full!

*****

March 25, 1885

Jacob Thaddeus arrived a few weeks earlier than expected, at 8:15 a.m. today. I thank the Lord that we both managed to come through the difficult labor. This time, Thaddeus had to help, as there was no Bethanne to act as midwife. Our new baby is very thin and scrawny and cries all the time. I believe he was too anxious to join this world and wishes he had remained in the warmth of my womb a bit longer.

Helen is walking now but remained remarkably quiet and inert during the hours of noisy pain I endured. She fell asleep finally in her little bed and missed the final drama of Jacob's emergence into our family. I believe she is quite bewildered by the existence of another human being now resting in her former cradle. I must put my pen aside to tend to Jacob, who has started to cry after only a few minutes of sleep. What is it about that insistent call that stirs within me the most urgent response? It is unlike anything I think people who have not given birth can comprehend. I must go to him.

*****

Although she had seen the next entry on her first read-through, Leah now noted the abrupt shift and then had to put the diary down as she read the next few words.

*****

May 13, 1865

We buried our precious Helen today, even as Jacob fed at my breast. How do I survive?

Chapter Twenty-Five

August 10, 1865

As I pick up my pen to record the truth of my daily life in this remote wilderness, I am struck by the realization that I have not written any words on these pages for almost three months. I know as I examine the harsh truth of those last words I inscribed on May 13, that the rounded contours of my penmanship, even in grief, belie the horror behind them. I have not written since because I could never have found words enough to express my grief nor the truth of my feelings since I awoke that morning to find the body of my darling daughter stone cold in her little bed at the foot of ours. We will never know what took her from us without explanation in the middle of a chilly night nor does it matter. All I know is that the light she brought me is unexplainable, and the hole that is within my heart is still too large to define with paltry phrases

I record my thoughts today only because it is warm, Jacob sleeps after a long and fitful night of colic, and because I need to count my blessings, and this diary is a testament to the things I have. I want my children and heirs to know that they had a strong family inheritance, one of fortitude and faith. I hope that somewhere years hence a young woman may pick up these pages and find that her mother or grandmother left a true account of one woman's life.

I do not foresee any time when women will not suffer as I have. If one dares to live fully, one encounters risk. What I want my daughters or the daughters of my offspring to read is that I grew in faith and strength from the ordeals which I encountered, and that they can, too, even though it is harder than I can imagine that I can surmount this pain.

So today, I will count my blessings. They are simple but welcome. Today I have a solid roof over my head in the midst of glorious nature. The summer sun shines on fields that Thaddeus and Billy planted and are harvesting as I write this. I found wildflowers rampant in the field next to my front door and am determined to remember their message of renewal.

We are actually finding that others nearby are joining our small but growing community, and although Billy has not found a wife, there is a family building a modest home only a mile from here. Just yesterday, I met the wife, whose name is Anna. She looks to be about my age and, although she does not have any babies yet, talks quite gaily about her envy of my having a son and of her plans to eventually breed many strong children. I did not feel it necessary to dim her optimism by sharing my recent loss. She and her husband are from Minnesota. I am excited at the prospect of another woman within walking distance. That is a blessing I dare not have requested.

And then, most special of all, is the news that Ingrid is on her way west to join us. She has the relative luxury of crossing by stagecoach instead of by wagon train. We were hoping she could come by the transcontinental railroad, but she did not want to wait for its completion. She should arrive here by mid-September. I can hardly contain my desire to see her again, though I know it must pain my parents to say goodbye to yet another daughter. Who could have imagined both the Sundborg girls would spend their lives at the edge of the frontier wilderness instead of tatting antimacassars in Boston?

And finally, I must express my gratitude for Jacob. His tenure on earth has been fraught with illness, causing much fear on my part, but he has not succumbed and grows stronger with each day. He's still tiny, but his belly is beginning to fill out.

So each day, I give my thanks to God for the mercies he has bestowed on us.

*****

(As I read this last passage to myself, I realize that nothing can adequately convey my true feelings. All of the brave words about future generations probably do not conceal my desperate grief at Helen's passing, but nothing can record the depth of my longing for her. There is not a single activity that passes in our home that does not stir my sense of loss. I think all the time about how Helen would be learning new skills or how much Helen would have enjoyed wading in the nearby creek on a hot Idaho summer day. I cannot look at her doll in its small cradle: was it just last Christmas that my life seemed so solid? Even as I nurse Jacob, the memories flood in of her sweet mouth at my breast.

I don't understand how women ever put to rest their pain and loneliness when a child dies. I will forever remember the fist clutching my heart, pain filling the void left by her laughter and touch. I know from seeing my parents' friends cope with suffering that it is a part of existence and a necessary experience for the gift of life, and my teachings and faith tell me that I should not question God's will, but in my deepest heart, I question the mercy of a god who would remove this precious child from my life. I am unable to believe in, much less utter, the religious platitudes with which I was raised. I was always told that God, in His infinite wisdom, knows best. Sometimes I want to damn, to blaspheme, that spirit. Does God have to be this impartial, this callous, or, even as I think these thoughts and fear for my soul, this cruel?

I know that time will help and that the needs of caring for Jacob and the other babies that I am sure are yet unborn to me will fill my hours with such immediate demands that the image of my firstborn will not be as fresh as it is now. Maybe someday, I will not see a shaft of light from the late afternoon sun and picture it glowing on her fine curls. Yes, I know that I may someday understand that my life is not mine to control, but that instead, I am a vessel of God's will, but truly now I just want her, my Helen. I don't want theology or pale words or creature comforts. If I am to meet her in heaven, as my Bible tells me, then why am I denied her presence now? I want her soft round arms around my neck, I want to hear her high voice as she giggles over my peek-a-boo game with her, I want to kiss the warm folds behind her ear, smell her infant sugar and spice scent. I long for my Helen. I almost cannot bear the pain.)

*****

Leah pulled her car up to the salmon-colored stucco sheriff's station in Miners' Rest, the county seat. She took only a moment to reflect how much time it must have taken Linnea or Thaddeus to travel to what came to be their town when it grew to accommodate the merchants and visitors associated with agriculture, not mining. Even though the trip must have become simpler as adequate roads were built, it was not a journey made lightly every day if one forgot to buy the right color thread at the mercantile. Now she understood why Esau eventually sold off much of the land around the cabin and then abandoned it after his parents' deaths. His thriving law practice in Miners' Rest demanded he make the trip in every day, a daunting task, especially in winter. Only later did Prospect become a town big enough to support an attorney.

Now it seemed like nothing, especially as the town and farms had blended into a county area almost continually dotted by homes close enough to chat with neighbors on a whim. The cabin still occupied a slightly remote spot because of its proximity to Bureau of Land Management land and US Forest Service territory.

The temperature was especially hot outside in the early August afternoon, and so Leah appreciated the cool relief of the air-conditioned interior. She made a mental note to keep all the cabin windows open tonight before she packed tomorrow in the hope of containing some of the cooler night air.

She noticed that only one secretary was seated in the three-desk area behind the high counter. She stepped up and, when the slight brunette looked up, announced herself.

"Hi. I'm Leah Brown. I'm supposed to file a report on an incident last night."

"Oh, hi! Sure. Just a minute. Let me get one of the men to help." The young woman walked to the rear of the building and returned with a burly middle-aged man in a uniform; he sported the largest black walrus mustache she'd ever seen. She couldn't imagine that adornment being accepted in a big city police force. Somehow it reassured her, and she felt calmed as he approached.

"Hi, ma'am. I'm Officer Wallace. Pleased to meet you." He extended his hand. "Sorry you had to go through that last night. I hope you're OK today."

Leah was impressed with his smooth manners. She asked him about the forms she would have to fill out, and as he handed them to her, she waited until he finished explaining the process, and said, "Tell me, please. Where is Moose? I mean, is he here? What will happen to him?"

He shrugged his shoulder toward the back of the building. "He's back there. We have a couple of holding cells." He turned his attention back to her, noting her reaction. "Don't worry, though. He can't hurt you."

"What's going to happen now?" Leah asked

"Well, it depends. You know, old Moose there really wouldn't have seriously hurt you, especially since he was unarmed. We've gotten used to his rantings and ravings. Truth is, most tourists through here don't get up to where he is. But he did scare the bejesus out of you, and I understand if you decide to press charges."

Leah thought about this for a moment. She certainly didn't want him out there scaring and stalking other innocent people. But then again, she felt as though she had not really been harmed. Somehow in the light of day, she didn't feel outrage. Instead, oddly, she felt pity for the huge round figure of a man who didn't fit into any of society's prescribed squares.

"I don't know. I have to think about it. Can I be sure you will keep him here until I leave tomorrow? If there were some way I could be sure he wouldn't do this again, I'd forget the whole thing."

She completed the report and handed the papers to Officer Wallace, wondering, in a random manner, how he kept his mustache free from food particles.

"Well, OK, then. Thank you, ma'am. We'll get back to you about the next step. Right now, Ol' Moose is still sleeping it off. I doubt he'll even remember what happened last night. He could probably ask for representation and try to get bail, but he's indigent, so I don't think he will. He's the kind of guy who doesn't mind staying in here for a few days, as long as he gets his three meals. The county prosecutor is coming in today, though. Chances are he'll want to talk with you. Is this number here your cell phone?"

He looked at the information on the first page of the report.

Leah confirmed the number and told him she would be available to talk with the prosecutor any time. She felt queasy and calm at the same time. Was it because she didn't want to hurt that man? She sensed that he was mentally unbalanced, probably deserved some treatment and loving care. And yet he'd caused her to flee in absolute panic. If not at his hands, she could have been seriously hurt by tripping in the dark.

She sensed that her unease also had to do with the reality of his presence in the world, of his rage and sadness and bulk interfering with her more law-abiding and logical existence. His life was in chaos, yes, but what would she be like cut off from the requirements of civilized relationships and of the loving concern of others? She wouldn't be a Moose, that she knew, but she had certainly not been entirely noble these past few weeks in her own pursuit of a break from reality. The line might be finer than she wanted to consider between those who violated moral edicts and those who violated laws or the space of other people. She thought about her mother's alcoholism and her father's leaving his family through suicide. She did not feel quite as certain as she might have before succumbing to Adam's charms of her upright position as a woman of conscience and morality.

She thought of Truman Capote's description of one of the killers in *In Cold Blood*. His face, according to Capote, looked as though it had been cut in half and then the two parts put back askew so that his facial features didn't quite fit together where they should. Of course, the burden of his appearance was no excuse for his complicity in the slaughter of innocents, but it did give one pause in attempting to understand the misfit mentality. Moose was a misfit. Even though she understood that, she didn't want him harming others. How much should she take on the responsibility for determining his fate?

Chapter Twenty-Six

September 29, 1865

My beloved Ingrid is here at last! Two days ago, I was shelling peas on the front stoop of my home with the late afternoon heat warming my face, when I saw two riders emerge in the distance similar to the Idaho desert mirage when I had to abandon my chest of drawers. As they came closer, I noticed that one of them rode sidesaddle and was attired in a skirt. The closer the riders came, the more I felt my heart pounding with anticipation. I almost didn't dare to think the female rider could be Ingrid, but as I have looked every day for this sight, I began to hope wildly that it was so. Finally I heard the distant pounding of hooves and a voice whose words were unintelligible but whose tone was familiar, Ingrid calling to me. I confess that I stood up, letting the shelled peas fall from the folds of my skirt, and ran down the path in front of our door. In just a flash, the horses pulled up, and I was able to grab Ingrid's skirts as she dismounted.

"Linnea, Linnea," she said.

Both of us were crying and exclaiming and holding on to each other as though if we held each other tightly enough, we would never be parted again.

Last night, we shared our dinner meal as a true family—Ingrid and Thaddeus and Jacob and I, and I felt some healing *toward being whole again. In fact, I think it is the first time since Helen died that I glimpsed the prospect of a measure of contentment, allowed a smile to crease my face and, under the guise of relief at Ingrid's safe arrival, felt I could cry out loud.*

My sister has become more stout and more matronly since last we met. I believe that she has settled into a view of herself as a spinster. Selfishly, I am glad she has thus reconciled herself to being a helpmeet to us in Idaho, but at the same time I am sorry for her dashed dreams of romance. The thought that I will never again have to face my life without her succor is of more comfort than I dare to imagine. I am beginning to become superstitious enough that I will not dwell on my good fortune. I am afraid that one of the powers that be will hear my delight and find reason to snatch it away from me.

Thaddeus is also pleased. He has always cared for Ingrid, and now I think is a bit relieved that he will be aided by her presence. I can express to her those feminine concerns that he barely has time to listen to. Of course, she will also be a help to me and to our endeavors as a family to make this land fruitful and our lives meaningful.

Thaddeus fixed up Billy's former room with a new bed and removed part of two logs to create a high window for her. I presented Ingrid with a quilt I made from scraps of fabric I had left from sewing projects these past few months. I don't know if she wishes to hear that four of the squares are remnants of fabric I used in making a pinafore dress for Helen's first birthday. As I stitched them, it somehow didn't make me sad but grateful that at least they would warm another one I love.

*****

October 6, 1865

    Last night, we had a small party in celebration of my sister's arrival. I invited Billy and his friend who had brought Ingrid to us from Miner's Rest (and stayed to help Billy for a few days) and our new neighbors Anne and her husband, Jeremiah. Jeremiah surprised me in his appearance. He towers over all of us and is possessed of a massive amount of curly black hair on his head and a beard and mustache of rich texture and thickness. He has rather merry-looking blue eyes, which peek out from between his beard and heavy eyebrows. He claims to be of Creole heritage, having worked his way up the Mississippi to seek his fortune and winding up so far north that he finally settled into work as a blacksmith in Anna's hometown. I would like to find out more about him. I imagine most of the settlers we will encounter have similarly interesting backgrounds. We do, I think, share a thirst for adventure and challenge that means most of us (I being the exception in that I would have stayed in Massachusetts if given the chance) have come here for dramatic reasons and thus share dramatic natures. I look forward to my exploration of this mixed citizenry!

    We roasted a fat chicken, and Ingrid and I prepared a dish of fresh potatoes cooked in their skins over an open fire. We also had peas and the most delicious apple pie that Anne baked. It was a festive occasion, interrupted only by Jacob's insistent cries. Ingrid, dear sister, was able to relieve me occasionally by rocking him to his short periods of sleep. I am blessed.

*****

(Now I wish I could write down what happened after our four guests left and Thaddeus went to bed, but what my sister and I shared is too personal to be shared with anyone else.

Ingrid and I whispered while we washed dishes. We took the buckets outside so we could enjoy the star-filled, clear night. The evening air was filled with the scent of licorice from the wild plant near my door, and except for the absence of my darling Helen, I felt at peace. But as I sit here reflecting on the busy few days since Ingrid's appearance, I realize that I am not as sorry about her spinsterhood as I should be. I know that she has a sense of lost dreams—she as much as told me so in our talk tonight.

"Linnea?" she said to me, with that open and honest look of inquiry I have adored in her so evident now on her face in the light of the kerosene lamp and the quarter moon. "Tell me, please, what it is like to know a man."

If it hadn't been a dim light, I would have thought she blushed.

"What do you want to know?" I said, realizing that I was placing on her the burden of opening up talk about difficult things.

"Oh, you know. To lie in bed with a man, to have his children...all the things Mother and Father would not discuss with us."

I thought for a few seconds before my reply. I wouldn't lie to her, but I did not want to be unfair to Thaddeus, either. In a flash came the memory of the night at the fort when I had loved Thaddeus with such passion. Was that really such a short time ago? How should I communicate the truth?

"Well, Ingrid. I guess I can say that sometimes it's wonderful. I mean, being close to someone you really love is how I think God meant us to be as men and women. And there are times when I truly enjoy leaning up next to Thaddeus's strong chest and inhaling his masculinity. Do you see what I mean?"

"Yes," she replied while she scraped the hard edges of potato skins off Billy's plate. "But what about the other times?"

"Well, I guess it's like life in general. There are days when we appreciate what we have and days when we don't. Marriages have bad and good moments, too." I looked at her and blurted out the rest. "There are times when I don't want Thaddeus to touch me."

When I saw the dismay on her face, I hastened to add, "I don't mean by that, dear Ingrid, that I don't love him. I do. But sometimes, the relations of a man and woman get clouded by other things."

She still looked downcast, so I continued, "What I'm trying to say is that to be honest, I think that our romantic fantasies as young girls don't always reflect the realities of marriage. It's just one of the things that we as grownups have to face." I paused as we gathered up the now dried plates and carried them inside, "So I don't want you thinking that you have somehow missed out on the greatest event that can happen to you as a woman. There are other pleasures that last and provide warmth and love, and I'm sure that life will hold them for you."

I felt shabby at saying these things, but Ingrid seemed to just shrug and then still gave me a warm hug before she went to her room. But after she left, I sat in the rocker for a long few minutes while I remembered what I had said to her. Behind my words was an unspoken thought. She's lucky. She doesn't have to get pregnant and bear the pain of child-birth and then love the child so much that the taking away of that love is worse than the severing of an appendage. She's lucky she will never know the ripping pains of birth and then the agony of love wrenched from her soul. She's lucky. Even though she might prefer the choice of experience, she's lucky to have an untouched womanhood.

I know my temporary bitterness is unkind and, I hope, uncharacteristic, but then being with child once again, as I am now, is not a choice I would have made.)

Chapter Twenty-Seven

August 9, 1998

L eah stretched and then lay on the floor for a few minutes, practicing some yoga exercises she had learned as a means of slowing down and taking the time to heal. As she worked on deep breathing, air filling her abdomen, then being released up through her diaphragm and out her mouth along with the toxins in her body, Leah looked up at the rough-beamed ceiling of the cottage.

She pictured Linnea and Ingrid working together under the same ceiling, keeping their voices low if Thaddeus were present or the baby asleep. She let her imagination wander to seeing herself included in the conversation, then arose and walked out to the small stoop in front of the cabin. Here, the women had washed dishes and confided their deepest thoughts to each other.

She yearned to read Ingrid's mind, understand the disappointments of her incipient spinsterhood, the feelings she must have had at her sister's bald words. What hopes had she fostered of courtship, perhaps even of romance out here near her sister? Were they so drastically different from the dreams of the teenagers Leah observed flirting in the malls of the Bay Area? Oh, perhaps they took a different shape, but most young girls always, Leah bet, wished for a Prince Charming.

There was time later in life to deal with the realities of knowing a man's faults, of accepting the limitations imposed by human frailty on love and marriage. Did Ingrid ever marry?

She felt the late afternoon sun burning the back of her neck and moved out to the grove of trees north of the cabin. Still standing was the cold cellar Thaddeus must have built to keep the potato crop, the foundation of two other small outbuildings, and a path which Leah had first explored five weeks earlier. She walked down it again now, eager to look at the few simple markers in the family cemetery.

As she approached, she tried to recreate the feelings of her ancestors as they carried a small body to an early grave. Leah remembered seeing two gravestones, although she knew that Linnea and Thaddeus were buried in the cemetery in Prospect.

Leah sat back against the thick trunk of the old cedar tree. She felt a heavy weight in her chest. Now questions assailed her. She knew she was at end of the diary; only a few pages were left. She wished for more. What had happened to Jacob? He must have survived, at least through this third Milton birth. Were there others? If so, why hadn't Leah ever heard about the rest of the Sundborg-Milton clan? How much grief had Linnea experienced as she buried her second daughter too soon after Helen's death? She studied the graves more carefully. Each had, in addition to its marker, a cluster of small stones set firmly in a circle. The stones reflected the landscape of the clay-like soil around them. Leah imagined Linnea placing them there, symbolic of—what? The answer whispered: a circle of love.

The afternoons must have been chilled here in this sacred place so long ago, with Idaho 's springtime cold. Leah felt her bones ice even as the sun blazed behind her.

Chapter Twenty-Eight

The tea soothed. She rested back into the comfort of the lumpy sofa and picked up Linnea's diary.

December 12, 1865

Today, as Ingrid and I were finishing the baking for Lucia Day and chattering about the prospects of a true Swedish smorgasbord this Christmas Eve, we heard cries above the crackling of our scented fire. When both of us rushed to a window, we saw Billy astride his horse holding a limp person on his lap. Through the light snowflakes, we could discern the long dark braid of a woman outlined against the white flanks of his horse.

While I put Jacob down on his blanket, Ingrid had already rushed into the cold day. I could hear agitated cries, and even as I was grabbing my coat to join them, Ingrid, Billy, and the girl he was carrying came into the cabin. I rushed to find a blanket for her but then just motioned to them to put her on our bed. Thaddeus was out in this bitter winter day, making some repairs on the fence so far out of my sight that I couldn't call him, and I guess that he hadn't seen Billy arrive, because he didn't ride up at any time during the next few hours while we learned the story of the girl Billy brought to us.

As Ingrid started heating water, I took off the cumbersome outer garments of what now appeared to be a young Indian woman. She was breathing, though very lightly, and was in a deep sleep. She had numerous cuts and bruises around her face.

I turned to Billy and asked him how and where he discovered her.

By now, Billy had taken off his jacket and hat and pulled up a stool near the bed. He gazed up at me with an expression of fear and loathing.

"I don't know if I should tell you. It's gruesome," he said, averting his glance from mine.

"Please, I can hear anything. Remember, I'm one of those who regularly visited the Bone Express on the Oregon Trail. I'm not afraid of blood," I replied.

"All right, then. Well, this girl here is a member of the Nez Perce tribe." Billy paused, saw that I knew his reference, and continued, "She showed up in Miner's Rest a couple of weeks ago, so I'm told, with a young fellow who had been out here from Pennsylvania for a couple of years trying his luck at the mines. Name's Blake. Seems he doesn't have a particularly respectable reputation."

By now, the girl was moaning slightly, and I took a cool cloth and put it on her brow. I noticed that her hands were dirty, with nails caked and black. She had crusted clumps of some kind of debris in her hair and above her eyebrows. Her clothes were made of a scratchy brown wool and sewn together crudely. She had on boots that were worn through in places. I decided to remove them as gently as I could while Billy continued.

"Her name is White Bird. Apparently, Blake arranged for her purchase in marriage a few weeks back and dragged her to Miner's Rest with him. I'd guess she's about fourteen."

The girl winced as Linnea pulled the left boot over her ankle.

"So what happened to Blake? Why did you find her in this state?"

"Best I could piece it together from Bethanne and others was that he'd get drunk every night and hit her around a bit. (They were staying at the hotel.) He was waiting for some money that was supposed to arrive on the Pony Express. Anyway, she pretty much stayed in their room all the time and wouldn't even let Bethanne in to check up on her, so after a week or so, Bethanne gave up. She's busy enough as it is. You know, the worse the mining is, the wilder the people are who are still left around. You wouldn't recognize Bethanne. She's really worn out. I think they'll get out of the business soon."

"So go on. What happened to get her beaten this badly?"

By now, I had undone the girl's blouse and felt around her waist. She had some pretty severe cuts and bruises there, too, and Ingrid and I set to cleaning them up.

"Finally, yesterday, just when I arrived in town, so did the Pony Express. Guess they left a packet for Blake and it was delivered to his room. But when he came home and went into his room, the packet was gone, and White Bird was asleep. He started beating her and yelling that she'd stolen his packet, wanting to know where she hid it. She kept denying it, but finally we all heard him slam the door, so we couldn't really make out what else was going on. It was awful quiet. I didn't see or hear anything more, so I went to bed.

"Turns out, some rabble rousers who had been drinking it up and listening to the fracas had run out behind the hotel to see what was going on. Blake had tossed her out their window and those guys just found her and did everything you can imagine to her. This morning, I heard people talking about a lynching party and how they were going to get some squaw. I didn't think there was anything I could do about it, but I decided to look for her. It had started snowing a little, which made it harder for me but probably better for her to hide in. Anyway, I did find her on the edge of town, huddled up behind some hay *stacked near the livery stables. She wasn't awake, so I just threw her on Rusty and here we are."*

I couldn't believe my ears, but the more we uncovered of this unfortunate woman's condition, the more despair I felt at what I had heard was the lawlessness of Miner's Rest, and the ache in my heart increased with each wound I bandaged.

She is resting now in our house, and I must return to my chores. We will find some shelter for her.

*****

December 13, 1865

Our little dove, White Bird, spent a fitful night but recovered enough to make the journey on horseback with Billy to Anna's house. Thaddeus did not like the young Indian woman's presence in our home for many reasons. First, as he clearly pointed out, we have little room here, especially as Ingrid has the spare bed. Truthfully, though, he was fearful that some sort of posse or band of renegades might come to seek her. They know where we live but are not as clear about Anna and Jeremiah's whereabouts. Billy said he would be glad to see her safely there, and White Bird did seem fine about it. My hope is that she can be returned to her tribe. I doubt that her husband would dare to go there to get her since it is clear he has mistreated her. I know the Nez Perce are peaceful people, but I am sure they would not welcome someone who had beaten one of their women.

So the girl's fate is out of our hands for the time being. I would like to learn more about the customs of her people. What frightens me is the prevailing attitude that says all Indians are savage and war-like. I know her tribe has been most agreeable in allowing settlement on their territory, and I do not think it is fair to liken them to the fabled Apaches and Sioux. We have had nothing but friendliness in the times we have encountered the Nez Perce.

Once again, I am plagued by nausea with my pregnancy. I am fortunate to have Ingrid around to help me with my chores. Now that the days are shorter, we will spend a great deal of time together indoors. She brought with her another trunkful of books, and I am excited about reading together after dinner on the long, cold nights.

*****

The knock on the door was firm. Leah put down the journal and her tea and went to the door. Adam stood there, his hand behind his back like some caller hiding roses. Leah didn't particularly feel like talking to him at this precise moment but asked him in anyway.

She found herself saying, "Please, come on in. It's good to see you," and in spite of her first reaction, she thought that, yes, it was good to see him. He looked a bit tired, with some shadows under his eyes, but then she guessed that he hadn't slept well. He looked as outrageously handsome as she had thought the first time she met him. That hadn't changed.

He entered the cabin with his arms still concealed behind him.

"Thanks," he said. "Here. I have something for you." He brought his arms around to the front and there was her father's tackle box. "I have your fishing rod and whatever else I could find in the car."

Leah went over to him and took the box, placed it on the kitchen table, and then, turning back to him, said, "I don't know what to say. How did you find this?"

She was aware that the question seemed fatuous; none-theless, she awaited his answer.

"I went back up at the first light of dawn today. The sheriffs described the spot where they found Moose, so it wasn't too difficult to locate. Anyway, as I recall, it's near one of the bends in the river where we saw each other earlier this summer. I knew how much this meant to you, as something from your father and all."

"Oh, yes, Adam. Thank you so much!"

She went to him now and let herself be enclosed in his embrace. Before she knew it, she was sobbing, and Adam led her back to the sofa. They sat and she leaned into his strong arms.

"Please excuse me," she said. "I'm really happy you did this for me. It means more than you'll ever know."

As she said this, Leah understood the subtext of these words. Yes, it meant so much because it had been a last gift from her father, but it also reminded her that the man with whom she'd experienced a brief night of passion was truly a good person. In spite of her rudeness to him last night, he had thought of her and taken the time to retrieve something precious to her. She turned to him now, wiping her nose with a tissue from her pocket.

"Adam, I want you to know something."

"Oh, oh. Doesn't sound good. Am I going to get the 'you're-so-nice-but' speech?"

Leah smiled in spite of herself.

"No, not really. First I want to apologize." She pulled away from him now, moving farther toward the west end of the couch.

"What for?" Adam seemed genuinely puzzled.

"For kind of dismissing you last night. I know you meant well, to offer to stay here and all, but I just thought it would be best if the sheriffs stayed here, not you."

"I think I understand. But can you tell me why?"

"Well, first on one level, they kept calling me Mrs. Brown, and I just didn't want them thinking things about why you would stay here. Also, their reference to me as somebody's wife did remind me of the impropriety of your being here. But," and here she paused, mustering up the courage to say this in just the correct way, "I realized that also I didn't want you pulling the strings. My life is my own, I am a responsible adult, and I have been too dependent on Ned and then, in this instance, you, to shelter me and protect and take care of me. I've been resenting Ned for his protectiveness, and here I was getting the same thing from you. I just felt like it tainted what we had had and made me feel helpless, like I'd somehow been seduced by a big strong man and wasn't a big part of the transgression. Of course, I was. I've rambled on, but do you see what I mean?"

Without giving him time to reply, she continued her rush of words. "I looked at you as someone I chose to violate my marriage vows for, as a relatively independent woman freed from constraints I'd felt all my life. That made it more special, you see. Something I'd elected to do, looking you right in the eye. Your taking over last night was a reminder that I am still weak in so many ways. I didn't want you to take over. That's Ned's job, not yours. And Ned has paid his dues. He's more entitled to boss me around than you are!"

She saw the dismay on his face, hated herself for saying too much. "Don't you see? You aren't that much different from Ned, only with Ned, I have children and a life and the kind of home that we have built. You need your freedom, I can sense that. But I need to be taken care of by the man who knows me more deeply than does anyone else in the world. And I, in turn, need to resume my role as a mother who takes care of her sons, who will not abandon them."

The sight of her father's tackle box on the coffee table was a vivid reminder of the loss she had felt at her father's absence and subsequent death. It was like a Jiminy Cricket in wood. She recalled the child who had vowed never to leave her children so alone.

She awaited his reply. He looked at her for a long time, leaned over, and gave her a rather brotherly pat on her thigh.

"Wow," he said. "I was only trying to help. But that's OK. I had a suspicion that you would return to home and hearth. I was feeling pretty squeamish about being involved with a married mother of vulnerable boys anyway. If we had time, I'd tell you about my early life and how I was about the same age as your sons when I was left behind in the wake of my mother's tumultuous affair with—I know it's a cliché— our pediatrician. Funny thing is, I'd vowed never to be guilty of that behavior, and here I am."

He stood up and headed for the door.

"But, boy. You *are* gorgeous. Don't ever forget your strength and the power of your soul. At the risk of acting too noble, I ought to say that I think it's time for me to pass on through this town. Maybe I'll find my little cabin somewhere else, maybe the Rockies. I've been thinking of Montana, somewhere near the Lolo Pass. Beautiful country, too! Enough space for all of us."

Leah remembered his words, "I'm a vagabond."

He touched the knob.

"I gather you're probably going to take this cabin off the market?"

"Probably. Yes. I don't think I want anyone else living in this house. My heritage, you know." *Our graveyard, too,* she thought. *A hallowed place.* Leah found herself standing up, going to him as he opened the door.

"Let me follow you out to the car. I'll get the rest of the fishing gear."

After he handed her the rod and reel and her creel, he turned away from her and got into the driver's seat. The window was down. Leah leaned in, so close as to see the yellow flecks of his eyes, the creases at their edges, to smell the woodsy scent of his hairline. She kissed him.

"Thank you, Adam."

She turned away, her cheeks blazing with a mixture of lust and pain and regret, and went into the cool of Linnea's cabin

Chapter Twenty-Nine

January 1, 1866

I *can hardly believe that it has been over three years since Thaddeus surprised me with a New Year's resolution to head out West. Even last year at this time, I was unsure that I would ever feel at home in this wild landscape, but I think I can fairly record that at last this does feel like home to me.*

Thaddeus is a happy man, though he is restless with the winter upon us. He occasionally sets out on horseback to check the property lines or to visit other families, so at least he has that freedom. I am housebound.

At least, Ingrid is here with me. It is amazing how many projects we can find to fill our days. We are sewing new blankets and quilts for the baby arriving in the spring and also for Anna, who surprised us yesterday with the news that she is expecting a baby this summer. Jacob may eventually have playmates!

Ingrid and I have set as our goal the establishment of a school. By the time Jacob is old enough to begin to read, we hope to have accumulated texts and materials for his education, and, the way we hear this territory is exploding with newcomers, we may even find that he will have classmates. Our dream is to include children from the Nez Perce tribe as well so that the concepts of democracy can be shared by all.

White Bird, who has settled in with neighbors some three homesteads away, has already promised to help us in these efforts.

Ever since the news that her husband was killed in a saloon brawl, she has come out of her hiding. (We thought we would never see her again when she traveled home to her family, but just a few days after we had given her up for lost, she returned to Anna, who had told her about the need of the new family for someone to help.) Now she seems like a sister to us. We hope she can be an interpreter when we start our school. It is a far-off dream, we know, but each time we are delivered of a parcel through the Pony Express, we add to our store of supplies.

In the meantime, I need to concentrate on my own health and that of Jacob, who, thank God, grows fatter and stronger each day. I think he is especially taken with his Aunty Ingrid and has flourished with her warmth.

Thaddeus is busy also with plans to build a bigger barn and to begin construction of a more permanent residence for our family. It may be years before we realize our plans, but I am encouraged that he looks so optimistically to the future.

*****

This was the last entry in the diary. Leah closed the journal with sadness. She yearned for more. Surely, Linnea had kept writing.

Inspired by this thought, Leah pulled over a chair. She still couldn't reach, so she moved the table over and stood on it and searched above the fireplace, hoping against hope that she had missed a companion diary on her first discovery. She could see back into the recesses of the space next to the chimney. The space was bare except for dust and a few bits of chinking.

She was so disappointed; she hungered to know more about her ancestors' lives and had many questions left unanswered.

Once she had read that Native Americans had a tradition of chanting the family tree. Thus, each generation knew the names of all their ancestors for six generations back. She wished that her family had been possessed of such a tradition.

She knew from family history that her great-grandfather Esau wasn't born until 1876, ten full years after this last entry. And she did not recall hearing about any great-uncle named Jacob. Had he, too, died before maturity? She longed to find out more about the ultimate fate of the Nez Perce girl, but that had not been supplied. What about the plans for a school? She recalled some mention from her mother about the one-room schoolhouse her grandmother Emily had attended in this area. Was it one founded by *her* grandmother Linnea? Linnea had died in 1892, but perhaps she had left the legacy of education for her unborn granddaughter, Esau's daughter, to enjoy in the next generation.

The phone rang, and Leah leapt up from the sofa, eager to speak with her mother.

"Mrs. Brown?" She recognized the drawl of the deputy sheriff, Officer Wallace.

"Yes?" she replied, with a keen sense of disappointment.

"I've got our county prosecutor here. He'd like to speak with you if you have a few minutes."

"Sure." she replied, then heard some shuffling of feet and papers in the background.

A surprisingly high-pitched voice came on the line. "Mrs. Brown? This is John Williams. How are you?"

"Fine," she said, and thought, *Not really.*

"I've been reviewing your statement and talking with the suspect. First, though, I understand you are returning to California soon. Is that true?"

"Well, yes. I'd hoped to, anyway."

"OK." He paused, trying to find the right words, she supposed. "In that case, I'd like to ask you to consider something I think might work."

"All right." She waited.

"I'm pretty familiar with this Moose character. His assault is a real departure for him. We have had reports about his language and yelling, his tirades. But he's never before touched someone. And he didn't have a weapon, as you know."

Leah interrupted. "I understand. But I didn't know that at the time. And he was very threatening."

"Yes, ma'am. That's true. And that's why we could really throw the book at him, felonies and all. If you want to press charges, we will."

"Yes?" Leah waited. She sensed that he was ready to propose an alternative. "What do you have in mind?"

"He is willing to spend some time in a work-release/ rehabilitation program we have up farther north. Kind of a plea bargain. And he will sign an oath, under pain of rigorous prosecution, that he will never return to these woods or harass people again."

When she didn't reply immediately, he continued, "You see? I think in this case, it just might work. He's pretty much at the end of his tether. Sobered up today, he was aghast at what he'd done. I actually think he does have a conscience under all that roughness. I think a program like this might work with him. If I didn't sound like a walking cliché for AA, I'd say he's hit bottom."

He waited. "Well, what do you think?"

Leah's reply was unplanned, came from somewhere right under the surface, as though she'd been waiting for it. "I guess I'll go with your best judgment on this. One part of me fears that he could harm someone else, but the other part of me thinks he should be given a chance. And I'm probably not going to be around to testify."

She didn't feel she had to tell him about Interferon and her disease.

"Well, then, that's what we'll do."

"I have one favor, though," she added. "I'd like you to send me a follow-up report on his progress or lack of it. And I want you—and him—to know that when I return here next summer, if I see any sign of him at all, I'll report him and let the law take its course. Is that clear?"

"Yes, ma'am. Perfectly clear."

She felt strong. "Good, then. I plan to bring my sons up here next summer and perhaps for many more summers, and I want to be sure it is the safe place I have always thought it to be."

"OK then. Have a good trip home."

As soon as Leah rested the phone on the table, it rang again. This time, it was her mother.

"Hi, dear. I found the information you wanted."

"Oh, great." Leah did not feel she needed to go into the events of the day, so she just waited.

"Do you have a pencil and paper?"

Leah opened her notebook filled with pamphlets and medical dispatches about hepatitis C and waited. "Yes, Mom. I'm ready."

"Here's what I found. Linnea recorded births and marriages only, not deaths. The person who inherited the Bible recorded only her death. Apparently, Linnea gave birth to eight children. Starting with Helen 1863, Jacob 1864, Bethanne

1866, Amanda 1867, twin boys, Samuel and Isaac, in 1869. Then there is a gap. Esau is born in 1876 and another daughter, Rachel, is born in 1877.

"On the same line, a marriage is listed. Ingrid Sundborg to William Willoughby in 1866. Do you know who he was, dear? They have no children after their name. Ingrid's line seems to stop with her."

Leah recorded the information about Ingrid, smiling inwardly. She did marry! Her fear of being an old maid was unfounded. Was William Willoughby *Billy*? How could she find out?

Her mother continued, "Then on the next line down, there is a record of only two of Linnea's children marrying. There are no death records for the others. Linnea's daughter Amanda married someone with a German name, Otto Gunter Schmidt, in 1910. There are no children listed as being born to them. I never heard about them, so I have no idea whatever happened to them. That entry and the one for Esau's marriage are in a different handwriting, and since they are listed there after Linnea's death in 1892, I assume your great-grandfather Esau's wife, Martha, must have recorded these."

Leah stopped her mother. "Mom? Just a minute. I'm trying to write all this down. It's wonderful. Now once again... Esau's wife?"

"Yes," her mother said, "Esau married Martha Garrison in 1906, and according to the Bible, they sired three children, Emily, your grandmother, born in 1910, Jacob, born in 1912, and Helena, born in 1913. I don't know anything about Jacob and Helena, so I presume they died before getting married to anyone. Does that help?"

"Yes, Mom. Thanks. I'll call you from home when I get there."

"OK, darling. Please drive safely."

Leah read again the names she had recorded. Of eight children born to Linnea and Thaddeus, only two were listed as married. Had they all died in their youth, or had a couple of them just not married and thus not been listed with the weddings? Leah had a horrible feeling that it was probable that the six children whose names were recorded only by Linnea had not survived to maturity. She burned to know.

Next summer, she would check county records for any listing of deaths. It would be a daunting task, but she had to know. She also wanted to research her family's contributions to this part of Idaho. She certainly would bring the boys up with her next summer. They could fish and explore the wilderness while she poured through resources at the county and historical libraries.

As thorough as Linnea's diary had been, it was still not enough. Her stories were remarkable, and so Leah was especially frustrated that she could not find a companion journal. She allowed herself to think that it was possible that Linnea had simply stopped writing with that last page.

Perhaps the pain of burying more children after Helen had just overwhelmed her. Could Ingrid have continued the family saga? Where were letters home? Perhaps she could search through the old trunks at her mother's and find out some more about her family.

Now she made a logical leap born of her frustration with the gaps in her family history. What stories would her sons or their children want to know about Leah's life? Would they find her experiences to be quaint and charming samplers of the lives of those growing up in the latter half of the twentieth century? How could she leave them a truthful sense of her life and lessons?

Whatever she recorded, Leah felt it had to be honest. If she died earlier than she might wish, she could at least let her children remember her span on earth by reading about it. Great-great-grandmother Linnea was no longer here, but Leah could sense part of her life as clearly as if she were telling her in person about it. She would never know the truth about the other women who had preceded her and passed without the benefit of a record of their experiences. Only her mother was still alive to tell the stories of her generation.

Suddenly, Leah had a sense of urgency about asking her mother to tell her stories. What was it like to be the first woman in her family to be divorced, to openly grapple with alcoholism, to leave her security and forge a new life for herself while she recovered from the loss of the one man she had loved? How did she experience loneliness, how did she deal with the complexities of a life seemingly easier than *her* mother's, at least in material conveniences, but harder—or at least different—because of the increased options and responsibilities of women in the latter half of the twentieth century? How had she felt, bereft and alone, meeting men who saw her as a "gay divorcee" and flirted with her without accepting the reality of her being a mother?

She wanted her mother to record these things, to speak in her own voice about her life, to give Leah a glimpse, now that she was a mature woman who could understand her mother's adult concerns, of the joy and sadness of being a woman in her time.

Leah decided to approach her mother about this, to share Linnea's diary with her and perhaps stimulate a response from her. She would ask her to write it all down or at least speak into a tape recorder about her history. At this moment, it seemed the most important gift her mother could give to her.

At the same time, Leah thought, as she sat staring at the closed diary in front of her, she could write her own history. No matter what her mother decided to do about her request, Leah could begin the process of sharing her life. She was infused with a sense of optimism. She would live to return next summer and learn more about her heritage. She would arise each day, in spite of Interferon, and record something, even if only a few words, about her experiences.

As Linnea had crossed the country to start a new life in alien fields, Leah had made her own way to a new life. Like Linnea's, hers was fragile. Determined not by her husband's dreams but by the exigencies of her illness, Leah had also, in a sense, to be a pioneer, to survive in her case oddly-named and often experimental new medicines and the pains of coping with her illness. Like her great-great-grandmother, Leah was a reluctant participant in her journey. She may have not chosen her path, but she could live through it with all the grace she could muster, as had Linnea.

She was tempted to put off the actual writing, to drive into town, buy a proper diary or journal covered in some lovely dimity or silk, but she decided instead to get right to it, to begin, this very minute. She would keep her thoughts in the notebook she had just used to jot down Linnea's Bible entries. She fixed a cup of tea, brought over a pillow from the sofa, and made herself comfortable at the kitchen table. The faces of her sons and husband, her mother and father and grandmother swam before her. She wished she had a picture of Linnea to use as an icon while she wrote. But then this was her story, Leah's. She began.

August 12, 1998,
Prospect, Idaho

To my dear sons Tim and Jeff:
 It is my hope that you will not come across these words for many years. That will mean that I have survived my illness and have spent lots of rich years with you both. I just want you to know that on this date, in the cabin built by my forebears over a century ago, I have decided to leave you an account of my life.

Leah placed the pen on the table, arose to move the shade lower in the hot August Idaho sun and, as she crossed the room, enjoyed the sensation of being truly at home, here, with her absent family and with herself. She imagined this dear place after some fresh renovation and maybe expansion to accommodate the people she loved so much.

 I am inspired by the words I have been reading this summer set down by my great-great-grandmother Linnea, who was just a girl when she and her husband left the comforts of everything they had known to follow his dream of homesteading in the West. I have realized in reading her diary what an amazing and determined woman she was. I trust you inherited some of her courage.
 I plan to share those words of hers with you over the next few months while I am recuperating. Perhaps some of the strength she had will rub off on me and will help me to get through this time. All I know is that whatever it takes, I am opting for any course of treatment which will increase the chances of my being on this earth a little longer than if I don't try them. The overriding thrust of my decision is based on my wish to see you both grown-up.

I hope that as you read this, you will be able to laugh at my sense of drama. "After all that," you may say, "Mom lived to be really old!"

Whatever happens, I want you to share with me the thoughts and emotions of a woman born in 1955, who experienced as a child the death of her father and all the conflicts of being a girl in the sixties and seventies. I'd like you to know how I met your father and fell in love with him and how we both cherished you, our sons. I hope that you will thus have a richer sense of the experience of women from your mother's generation but also of the realities for women of all times. For I do not think that I am so different from my wonderful Linnea. We both traveled a difficult path, had children, and experienced loss and responsibility and intense love, as I am sure your wives and daughters will do also.

So here it is, my darling boys, my testament, begun the night before I pack up and drive home to give you the kind of hugs I hope you are never too mature to welcome, to return to the arms of your father, who has supported me and loved me in a way few of my friends have known.

Tonight, I feel blessed, full of optimism and a kind of exultation, eager to count my blessings and give them back to you.

I love you both so.
Mom